THE LEADER'S GUIDE TO EMOTIONAL INTELLIGENCE

UNDERSTAND AND DEVELOP YOUR EQ FOR MAXIMUM LEADERSHIP IMPACT

DREW BIRD

Table of Contents

This book is dedicated to Maya. Thank you for making me feel like the luckiest man alive – every day.

Acknowledgments

Over the years, so many leaders have contributed to my understanding and learning of leadership that it would be impossible to name them all, but if you are one of those leaders, my heartfelt thanks to you.

I also want to thank my good friends John and Jason, who have both taught me so much about what it takes to be a great leader - as well as the true meaning of friendship.

Finally, I want to thank my editor, Gillian Katsoulis for all the help, advice, expertise, and wise counsel in putting this book together. I am quite sure that without her insight and persistence, this book would not have seen the light of day.

Introduction

In the past 26 years, I've had 20 different jobs in 15 organizations (what can I say, I get bored easily!). Some of those jobs were complicated and required specialized technical knowledge. Some were creative. Some were easy. None were as difficult as those where I was in a leadership position. Being a great leader is hard work. If you find it easy, my guess is you are not doing it right, or not doing it at all.

For the past decade. I have had the good fortune and privilege to work with leaders every day. I have sat with them, talked with them, planned with them, commiserated with them, celebrated with them, and dreamt with them. In some of these conversations, I was acting as a coach, in others as a confidant, a sounding board, a mentor, or a friend. The vast majority of these leaders weren't CEOs, the Top 40 Under 40, or Entrepreneur of the Year. They were people just like you and me – leading others every day, and trying to do the very best they can at it.

I have learned a great deal from these leaders. Much of the time, I stand in awe of their willingness to wrestle with the complexities of leadership. As they talk, I am often reminded of my own time in various leadership positions. Now, as a consultant, trainer, and speaker working with a group of associates and support folks, I get to lead people every day. I continually seek to develop my own leadership and strive to be a better leader.

When I think back to my early experiences as a leader, I wonder whether I was doing more harm than good. Back then, I was unconsciously incompetent. I didn't know what I didn't know. As is the way with many leaders, even today, I was given a leadership position but with no training, no leadership education, no courses, nothing. I literally had to figure it out as I went. You may have found yourself in a similar position at some point, or you are there now.

I won't say I did the best I could in that first leadership role because I wasn't paying much attention to the 'leading' part of the job. We had work to do. Everyone knew his or her role, but I understood that the buck stopped with me. When the brown stuff hit the fan (which was mercifully infrequent), we rallied around, figured out what needed to happen, and got it done. We were friends and colleagues. We worked together, went to lunch, laughed, and resolved the occasional conflict. But looking back, I can see that my leadership was what we call 'laissez faire', which basically means I just let things happen. I wasn't really leading at all.

As my awareness and knowledge of leadership grew, I became much more conscious of how my approach to leadership affected my actions and decisions. I was hungry for knowledge, so I would learn as much as I could about leadership. But putting my newfound knowledge into practice was more challenging than I thought. I knew what to do, but often struggled to do it.

At one point, I had an interesting dilemma. Two people in my department were creating problems. One, let's call her Sally, had been a friend, mentor, and support to me for the past few years. I cared deeply about Sally, but the reality was she was not doing her job. Sally deliberately did things against the customer's wishes, which meant that I was constantly trying to fix problems after the fact. Some clients even refused to work with her. We had many conversations about what was going wrong and what needed to change. We put things in writing. We followed the process. But in the end, I had to let Sally go. It was the hardest decision of my career by far.

The other person, who we will call Geoff, was causing problems within the group. Geoff was systematically alienating everyone around him, including me. He spread negative feelings about our department and our work throughout the office.

I should have let Geoff go for the good of the team, but during many of our conversations about his performance, he accused me of victimization and playing favorites. Geoff managed to manipulate my emotions to the point where I didn't fire him because I thought doing so would affirm his accusations. On some level, I think I respected Geoff for being disruptive at a time when I wanted to do more of that, and I also wanted him to like me. I am not sure why – he was quite an objectionable person.

It was a tough time for me as a leader. Of course I learned a great deal, but it was a tough time nonetheless. I reached out to other leaders, confidants, mentors, and coaches for support. It helped guide me in the right direction, but no one can lead for you; you have to do it yourself. And that means understanding what YOU are bringing to your leadership. Yes, leading by its definition involves other people, but it starts with you.

Like it or not, leading is first about what goes on in your head. Every action you take, every discussion you have, and every decision you make, every day, is a result of a chemical process most people barely understand. But we are beginning to understand that emotional intelligence – how we understand, manage, and act on emotional information – is a key component in effective leadership.

The role that emotions play in our behavior as leaders cannot be understated. Take, as an example, the scenario I described earlier. When I realized I had a problem with the Sally, I talked to Human Resources about the correct procedure for progressive discipline. It took me about 20 minutes to understand the process, and I could have pretty much recited the entire policy within 24 hours. The process, and the policy attached to it, were not difficult to understand.

Once I reached a point where I knew I had to let her go, it still took me over a month (and many sleepless nights) to make the decision to do it, and then another two weeks to get up the courage to actually have the conversation. Why did it take me so long? My emotions got in the way. And that's not necessarily a bad thing if I could have better understood and identified it.

With Geoff, I realized that I should let him go, but then moved no further. I delayed and delayed and put it off and avoided the issue, all while continuing to have performance discussions with Geoff that went poorly. Of course, Geoff may have been right – I might have been victimizing him – but Geoff levelled the same accusations of leadership inadequacy, victimization, and personalization at just about anyone who didn't agree with him on every point.

In the end, the organization restructured and Geoff went to another department to report to someone else who happened to be a good friend of mine. I apologized to this friend for not dealing with a situation that would now fall to her. Once Geoff was in the new department, he began accusing that manager of not understanding, not giving credit, and playing favorites. The adversarial cycle between Geoff and his manager started over again.

Geoff left the organization shortly thereafter. Some might say that my 'wait and hope' approach worked out in the end, but the collateral damage was significant.

I didn't do what needed to be done and the team, the organization, and I all suffered as a result. Most organizations have people like Geoff in them, and it is a common theme across organizations to simply not deal with difficult people. Part of the reason for that is that understanding what you should do in any given situation is one thing, but actually doing it is another. So what got in my way? I did.

We Are Both the Problem and the Solution

The human brain is a fascinating organ. Evolved over millions of years, it's an incredibly complex biological mass of cells, chemicals, and electrical impulses. But for all its complexity, the brain still operates on fundamental processes. One of the most basic of these is the 'fight or flight' response. Even though most of us don't have to determine whether to fend off a marauding horde or run from it, our brains are still wired as if we need to. When presented with a challenge, chemical processes in our brain will combine, collaborate, and scheme to tell us what we need to do. And because it's such a naturally embedded process, we often don't think too much about it. We just let it happen, kind of like breathing.

The average adult takes about 20,000 breaths every day. How many of those breaths are taken consciously? If you are like most people, you don't think too much about breathing. If you exercise regularly, or take part in yoga, you may become more conscious about your breaths during those activities, but for the rest of the time you are just breathing. In and out 20,000 times a day.

In a similar way, your brain operates in the background, always active. When you have to respond to external stimuli – be it something someone says, a physical interaction, or something you want to do – the brain makes it happen. However, it isn't purely based on logic. Your brain applies layers of feelings and emotions to your actions. It adds what we call 'meaning'. Sometimes, these emotions are strong enough, and noticeable enough, that you can pay attention to them and even name them. But for the most part, they are subtle. They filter information coming in – making you see what your brain wants to see – and color the response going out – making you say or do what your brain wants you to do.

So, when someone at work says, "Do you need some help with that?" while one person will hear it as an offer of assistance, another will see it as an accusation of inadequacy or incompetence. When someone else says, "Wow, that's fantastic," one person will hear it as a compliment, while another will hear it as patronizing or false. How we hear the message will depend on chemical process embedded deep in our brains, which are affected by situations, history, relationships, sleep habits, stress levels, hunger, and so on.

Tapping into and understanding how emotions play such an important role in our behavior is the essence of emotional intelligence.

What Can We Do About It?

I wrote this book to help leaders like you become more emotionally effective. Through my work with leaders in a broad range of settings and sectors, I have observed that certain skills predict the success of leaders more than others. Some of the key success factors I have seen in great leaders are:

- They have a level of self-assuredness without being arrogant or appearing over-confident.

- They are able to understand and manage their emotional reactions to internal and external challenges.

- They build healthy, differentiated relationships with their teams, peers, and their own manager.

- They confront difficult situations in a proactive, grounded manner accepting that, as a leader, they may have to make unpopular decisions.

- They handle stress well, acting as a role model to their own team.

As we will discuss in later chapters, management and leadership development programs often focus on developing skills in specific areas related to the items above. For example, they might cover areas like interpersonal communication, conflict management, employee engagement, or time management. But while there is a great need for these 'technical skills,' as I call them, if the leader's underlying emotional intelligence is not sufficiently developed or balanced, they will struggle to implement the skills they learned.

To provide a more practical example, if a leader learns conflict management skills, but tends to avoid dealing with emotionally difficult situations, the conflict management skills they have learned are unlikely to be used. But, develop the underlying emotional intelligence first and help the leader understand how they can become more comfortable in dealing with the emotions involved in difficult situations, and you create a platform on which the new skills can be applied.

Why Did I Create This Book?

When I work with leaders, there is often a strong understanding of how developing their emotional intelligence could positively impact their everyday activities. However, many are not certain how they can get started with that development. The good news is that developing EQ is as simple as increasing awareness of your thoughts, tendencies, and behaviors, and then undertaking simple activities to analyze and understand what's going on. Then, by taking small, concrete actions on a regular basis, you can begin to develop your EQ. The key is to keep on implementing these skills, week after week, month after month.

That's where this book comes in. By providing you with an overview of the role of emotional intelligence in leadership and explaining how you can develop it, I will provide a structure for your development, with simple activities and a little inspiration along the way. This book can be your ongoing companion as you develop your emotional intelligence.

While you can see results from this process very quickly, if you are looking for an overnight solution to developing your EQ, this book is not it. I don't know of one, but please feel free to drop me a line if you find it! This book is about taking a mindful, consistent approach to developing your emotional intelligence.

Who Is This Book for?

Most leaders and managers are working hard each and every day to support the members of their team to reach and surpass their objectives. The team may be small or large. It might be in a corporation, or a tire store, or a physician's office, or a police department, but the challenges are the same. Although there may be inherent differences in these groups, I have yet to meet a leader, team, or organization that couldn't benefit from increasing their understanding or application of emotional intelligence.

Before we get started, there is one important overriding element to this work that you need to be aware of and committed to. The most successful leaders and managers I know are the ones who are able to admit, up front, that they have as much – if not more – work to do on their own 'self' than the people they lead.

If your approach to leadership and management is that everything will be good once *other people* start doing what they are supposed to, then this is not the book for you. Yes, others may need to behave differently, or show up differently in the workplace, and you may be the one that can introduce them to that concept. But if you are not ready to accept that there are areas in which you may need to change, or improve, then I cannot help you. No one can.

How This Book is Laid Out

This book has three sections. In Section 1, we explore the role of emotional intelligence in leadership and what this 'emotionally effective leader' looks like on a day-to-day basis. At the end of the section, there are two homework activities. Of course you can complete them right away and move on, but you will get more out of them by taking a few days to reflect on the questions.

In Section 2, we look at emotional intelligence in depth and understand its roots, its evolution, and what it has become today. We also examine how and why it is so important to develop the entire range of your emotional intelligence rather than just focusing on one or two areas. Again, there is a homework assignment at the end of the section. Take some time to consider and reflect on it before moving on.

Lastly, in Section 3 we explore and understand how you can most effectively develop your emotional intelligence and create an actionable plan that you can use to sustain your EQ development over time.

I have also put together an online resources webpage, on which you'll find all the homework worksheets and additional resources that are mentioned in the book. You can access this page at: http://myeqcoach.com/lgeibook

I know your time is valuable, so I have made every effort to make the homework assignments efficient. I would strongly encourage you to do them. You will get more value from this book with them than without them.

Additional resources and exercises are available online at http://myeqcoach.com/lgeibook

Section 1

Leadership and Emotional Intelligence

1

Exploring Emotional Intelligence in Leadership

How do you view yourself as a leader? Do you think you are a good leader or a bad one? What makes someone a leader? In this chapter, we will take some time to explore these questions and delve deeper into what leadership really means.

We will start by looking at a basic model for understanding leadership, including a look at where emotional intelligence fits. Then we'll discuss how we, as leaders, risk falling into negative cycles of behavior, and how we can transform them into positive habits.

Good Leader, Bad Leader

Before we get into a deeper discussion of leadership and emotional intelligence, take a moment to consider what a good leader looks like to you. Please find a piece of paper and a pen.

First, draw a vertical line down the middle of the page, then a horizontal line about an inch from the top of the sheet. In the top left box, write "Good Leader," and in the top right, write "Bad Leader."

Take a minute to think about some of the best leaders you've worked with. Consider what made them good and how others responded to them. Now, set a timer for one minute. In the left-hand column, write as many positive characteristics of those leaders as you can think of.

Now, take a minute to consider some of the worst leadership you've experienced. What made them bad and how did you and others react to them? Set your timer for one minute again. This time, in the right column, write down some characteristics of these bad leaders.

Now take a moment to look at the two lists. What do you see? If you are like most people, you'll notice that the things you wrote down in both columns have to do with the way the leader interacted and treated you, how they supported and coached you, how they behaved on a day-to-day basis, how they contributed to the team or the organization, how they made decisions, and how they handled stressful or difficult situations.

You'll also likely notice that you didn't comment so much, if at all, about how those leaders did their own work, how good they were at the technical aspects of their role, or how much they knew about the business. You won't see references to the leader's project management skills or how good they were with spreadsheets.

The truth is that when it comes to evaluating great leadership, we tend to be much more interested in things like interpersonal relationships, teamwork, and collaboration, both for good and bad leaders. And all of these things are either a part of, or directly related to, emotional intelligence.

Characteristics of a Great Leader

An interesting thing about leadership is that often, the specific characteristics and behaviors you attribute to good leadership differ from one person to the next. However, chances are that your good leader list includes things such as:

- they understood me as a person
- they encouraged me to do my best
- they trusted me
- they were supportive
- they were clear about expectations
- they dealt with difficult situations
- they weren't afraid to address issues
- they were consistent in their behavior

These attributes, characteristics, and behaviors point to the importance of emotional intelligence in leadership. Being aware of those around you, and supporting them, will help build you up as a leader, while inspiring those around you to believe in you as well.

Before we move on, consider this: if you were to ask your team about the characteristics of a great leader and great leadership, would they think of you? What characteristics, behaviors, and attributes do you think they would list?

To be a great leader, start by being the kind of leader you would want to follow.

The Realities of Leadership

It's easy to think about all the things you should be doing as a leader, but before we go on, let's discuss some of the realities of leadership. Many of these are realities I learned the hard way while leading individuals, teams, groups, and departments. I work with hundreds of leaders as a coach, trainer, and consultant. With each one, these realities become clearer. The earlier you understand them, the easier it will be to take on a leadership role and succeed in developing your leadership abilities.

Reality #1: Great leadership is not easy

As I mentioned earlier, my experience tells me that if leadership is easy, you're either not doing it right or not doing it at all. Now I'm not suggesting that every day in a leadership role has to be a miserable slog. What I'm saying is that great leadership requires consistent effort, thoughtfulness, and a commitment to work at our craft. For most leaders, this is in addition to what may already be a heavy work load.

Reality #2: Leadership can be stressful

Many tasks and actions associated with leadership are difficult and require a leader to take actions that could create conflict or produce tension between themselves and their team, between them and their manager, or between members of their team. By its nature, leadership is a social activity that requires interaction with other people and as soon as groups of people work together, the potential for issues and conflict exists. Time and experience help leaders understand what they should and should not be concerned about when it comes to conflict management.

Reality #3: Most leaders are being asked to do more and more with less

It's a reality of our world that the demands on leaders and on their teams are constantly increasing. Pressure to be more productive and profitable and to produce higher quality results can create additional burdens for the leader. In many situations, a leader becomes the mediator and moderator for additional requests between their managers and their teams. It's no wonder that in his incredible book, *Seeing Systems: Unlocking The Mysteries of Organizational Life*, Barry Oshry refers to leaders who are answering to a more senior leader, and also to a team below them, as the *torn middle*. They are torn as they try to satisfy both parties who have different needs and desires.

Reality #4: Not all followers, or team members, care to be led

I have had other leadership coaches challenge me on this point, saying that a great leader will always find a way. In my own experience, and the experience of many other people I have worked with, however, I have learned that in some cases people simply do not want to be led. Sometimes these individuals will create toxicity in the group and in their relationships with you, and with other people in the organization. When this happens, serious action may be required. However, in many environments, all the leader can do is manage the toxicity and keep the damage in check. Organizational policies, union restrictions, or a lack of organizational support can prevent even the most effective leader from doing anything more than that. Of course, a leader should do everything they possibly can to manage such situations, but they must also accept that not everyone cares to be led.

Reality #5: Followers constantly evaluate the effectiveness of a leader

Just because you were doing great at the leadership thing last week doesn't mean that you're doing great this week, at least as far as your team is concerned. Being a leader is about working *with* your team to achieve whatever goals you've set. So, how people perceive your effectiveness on a day-to-day basis is important.

Some leaders will tell me that they don't care what their team thinks of them as long as the work is getting done. Even if I believed them, which I don't, it's a dangerous perspective. When people enjoy working with their leader, when they respect that leader and maybe even like their leader, they exhibit behaviors that they otherwise would not. This *discretionary effort*, as it is called, can lead to higher productivity and reduced turnover, both very concrete outcomes that every leader should care about.

Reality #6: If you have struggled in your leadership, you're not alone

As I mentioned before, I get to work with hundreds of leaders every year. If there is one common thread to the discussions, it's that most leaders want to do better in their role and many are often struggling with one or more aspects of their leadership.

It is a mistake to look at other leaders and assume they are doing a better job, with less stress, than you are. Many leaders compare themselves negatively to others, but if you are ever able to talk honestly with another leader, they may well tell you that they, too, have trials in their role. This is one of the reasons I am such an advocate of peer mentoring: it can be useful to know that you are not alone in your struggles.

Reality #7: Leadership CAN be developed

The last reality of leadership I want to share is that leadership *can* be developed. But it requires commitment.

The old debate of nature-or-nurture doesn't get much air time these days, and rightly so. I have known many leaders that seem to have lots of natural potential, but who never end up realizing it. I have also seen people who you might not initially consider to have much leadership ability develop into the most effective leaders you can imagine.

Here is the bottom line: if you're willing to make a commitment to understand and develop your leadership, you can become a better leader and deliver greater results. The challenge for many leaders is that they are not willing to put in the work required to reach their leadership goals. After all, it is a lot of work. But that work doesn't need to be onerous or miserable. Great leadership is a joyous and rewarding thing to both develop and provide to others. Best of all is that great leadership is an amazing gift that can increase the quality of your life, and more importantly, the lives of those that you lead.

Understanding Your Own Leadership

Now that we have gone through some of the realities of leadership, it's time to dive in to a deeper understanding of what contributes to your leadership behavior. To do that, I would like to introduce you to a simple model that we use to help leaders understand their leadership. As there are three layers to the model, we refer to it as the *pancake* model.

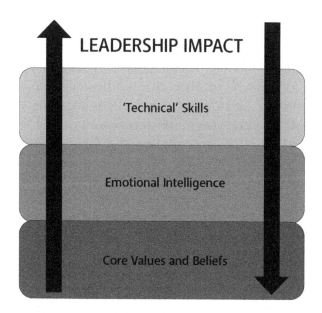

Underpinning your leadership are your core values and beliefs, which drive your behavior in every aspect of your life on a day-to-day basis. Sitting on top of the core values and beliefs is your emotional intelligence. At the top are your technical skills. In this context, we use the term *technical skills* to refer to the skills of leadership, like communication, change management, conflict management, or project management. They are not technical skills as you might think of them relating to IT or computers. Again, we will look at this in more detail later in the chapter.

Let's start our discussion by looking at the role of core values and beliefs in leadership.

Exploring Core Values and Beliefs

Core values and beliefs are foundational pieces on which your leadership is built. Understanding which values drive your leadership behavior is important, as it allows you to use those values as lenses through which you can take action or make decisions. For example, imagine that one of your core values is equality. With this value as a guide to your decision making, you can ensure that when you make decisions, you are choosing options that reinforce equality. Similarly, if one of your core values was honesty, you would ensure that you demonstrated honesty in all instances.

Identifying your values and then leading congruently with those values provides consistency in your behavior. Followers love leaders who are consistent.

Of course, there is a difference between practiced and aspired values. Just because a leader says they value something, doesn't mean that they are actually using that value in their day-to-day work. To become a better leader, you will want to act more congruently with your declared values – matching your practiced values with your aspired ones.

Mental models, or your beliefs, also shape your behavior, but in a different way. Your beliefs about the world influence your day-to-day leadership in significant ways. Understanding and, where necessary, challenging or changing your beliefs is an important part of your leadership development. Some beliefs are relatively benign. You may be aware of them or be willing to own up to them, and they may only influence your behavior in small ways. A positive example of such a belief is that everyone is a good person, or that everyone should be trusted until they prove to you otherwise.

Other beliefs can be more far-reaching and, in some cases, dark. For example, you may believe that women make better leaders than men, or vice-versa. You might believe that older people in the workforce are averse to new ideas, that young people don't take work seriously, that you can't relate to a certain group of people, or that a certain group of people may not be able to relate to you for whatever reason.

The important thing to remember is that it is not necessarily wrong to hold these beliefs. In fact, in many cases these beliefs have been formed and reinforced from your experiences, both good and bad. The key is to be as aware of them as you can. If you can take time to understand and acknowledge your mental models, you can do more to be aware of the effect and impact they may be having on your day to day leadership.

There are some mental models and beliefs about the world that you are likely not aware of – these are part of your 'shadow self.' Working to become more aware of them is a critical part of your leadership development. The famous psychologist Carl Jung pointed out that in the 'shadow' there can be both positives and negatives. Freud also noted that when it comes to being aware of our own behaviors, strengths, and areas for growth, "The you that you know is hardly worth knowing." For many people, this statement holds very true. We are not good estimators or identifiers of our characteristics, strengths, and opportunities for growth.

In the online resources section, you will find worksheets for both identifying your core leadership values and working to understand your underlying beliefs. These worksheets are designed as reflective activities to be completed over a period of time, rather than all at once. You won't need to have completed these exercises to continue reading.

The Role of Emotional Intelligence in Leadership

The next layer in our model is emotional intelligence. Emotional intelligence refers to a set of emotional and social skills that collectively establish how well we perceive ourselves and how we express our feelings, build and maintain relationships with others, understand our environment and make decisions, and deal with stressful or difficult situations.

We will dig into emotional intelligence in detail in future chapters, but for now this basic definition will suffice. If it helps, you can think of emotional intelligence as a filter through which all of your thoughts, actions, and reactions must pass, irrespective of whether that thought stays in your head, you say it out loud, or you act on it. Interestingly, the decision to keep it in your head or say it out loud is also a function of your emotional intelligence.

There have been many attempts to quantify how much of an impact emotional intelligence has on the effectiveness of your leadership. Multi-Health Systems, an assessment company based in Toronto, Canada, did a meta-analysis of all the available research back in 2002, and concluded that 80% of leadership effectiveness involved emotional intelligence. Eighty percent!

That One Thing

Daniel Goleman, one of the world's leading authorities on emotional intelligence, and author of the book *Emotional Intelligence: Why It Can Matter More Than IQ*, has called emotional intelligence the "sine qua non of leadership," which basically means the 'essence' or most important thing.

I know from my own work with leaders that when someone starts to dig into their emotional intelligence, they begin to understand themselves and their leadership on a different level. The exploration and development of emotional intelligence also supports them in using their technical skills to reach their desired outcomes. They move from simply knowing what to do in a given situation to actually doing it. And, when it starts to happen, leaders begin to see the results they have been looking for. A positive reinforcing cycle starts that supports even more growth. We will talk about these cycles later in this chapter.

Technical Skills

As I mentioned, the top layer of the pancake model is technical skills. In this context, when I use the term technical skills, I am referring to practical leadership skills. I call these technical skills, because as with any role, there are learnable skills that are relatively easy to acquire. They include communication, conflict management and resolution, change management, and project management, among others.

When it comes to technical leadership skills, the real question is this: yes, they can be easily acquired, but will they be applied?

Early in my career as a leadership development trainer, I would run workshops on these technical leadership skills. In some cases, the workshops included role-playing. Very often, leaders in these sessions were able to demonstrate amazing role playing skills, but when they returned to their workplace, they failed to apply those skills. The reason was their underlying emotional intelligence.

I don't want you to think that I am devaluing these technical skills. They are incredibly important in effective leadership and they have to be learned. However, without developing the underlying emotional intelligence, they will not be applied when needed.

The Mistake Many Leaders (and Organizations) Make

The mistake many leaders, and many organizations for that matter, make is that they spend a great deal of time, money, and energy developing these technical skills before they have done the work to underpin elements of emotional intelligence, core values and beliefs.

Many organizational leadership development programs focus heavily on the technical skills, while others include emotional intelligence at the same level as technical skill development. My work with leaders and organizations has shown that if you truly want to develop leadership effectiveness, you must do the work on the underlying emotional intelligence before you provide leaders with these technical skills. Even the most basic of technical skills can be put to very effective use when the emotional intelligence of the leader has been developed.

One of the simplest examples I can give is the skill of active listening. Active listening requires empathy, impulse control, and a value of interpersonal relationships. Without these three skills, active listening is hard, or in many cases impossible. Only when you can truly experience another person's situation or point of view, control your need to interrupt, and value the connection you have with this other person, can you actively listen to them. Empathy, impulse control, and interpersonal relationships are all elements of emotional intelligence. So it makes sense that developing emotional intelligence will support active listening.

Positive and Negative Reinforcing Cycles

I want to close out this chapter by looking at positive and negative reinforcing cycles. A reinforcing cycle is a pattern of behavior that repeats over and again, bolstered by the experiences you have each and every day as a result of your actions. Here is how these cycles work.

As you know from earlier in this chapter, core values and beliefs underpin your emotional intelligence, which in turn affects your ability and willingness to apply your technical skills. The same is true in reverse as well. Your ability to use, either successfully or not, your technical skills, will affect your emotional intelligence, and then also influence your underlying beliefs. Your beliefs, now impacted by your experience, will affect your emotional intelligence, which will in turn impact how you demonstrate your technical skills, and so on. The important thing to remember is that these cycles will have a significant impact over time. For positive reinforcing cycles that's obviously a good thing. But for the negative reinforcing cycles, that can be very bad.

For example, lets imagine we have a leader who suffers from Imposter Syndrome. Someone suffering from Imposter Syndrome believes they are not qualified, experienced or capable of doing the job they have. They think they ended up where they are by fluke and that at some point they will be 'found out' and lose their job. Although it might sound rare, it is actually much more common than you think, especially for leaders who are new to their position.

Imposter Syndrome erodes the leader's self-regard, making them less certain of their abilities. It also affects their assertiveness, as they may not feel comfortable speaking about an issue or situation because they don't believe they are capable of understanding the complexities of that situation. It will also affect their stress tolerance, because when things start to get difficult, the leader blames his or herself for the lack of competence or knowledge of what to do in a given situation.

Now, because they are not experiencing positive results, their faith in their technical skills is eroded, which affects their confidence, self-regard, and their emotional well-being, which then reinforces their core underlying belief that they are an imposter. This negative cycle can be very damaging for leaders.

Now consider a more positive scenario. A leader has a strong belief in their abilities. This bolsters their emotional intelligence, meaning that the leader will not avoid difficult situations or challenges to their leadership. With their strong emotional intelligence, they are able to effectively use the technical skills they have learned, which results in them having the impact they desired. Achieving positive results reinforces their belief in, and mastery of, their technical skills, which reinforces key aspects of their emotional intelligence, which in turn feeds their core belief that they are a capable and effective leader.

Of course, day-to-day leadership is a complex mix of many cycles - so many that its literally impossible to identify them all, but one of the first steps in development for any leader is to acknowledge which of these cycles are working in your favor, and which are not.

So, emotional intelligence is a key factor in building and practicing good leadership. One might argue it is the most important aspect as it affects how well a leader can employ their technical skills. Emotional intelligence impacts not only your relationships with others, but it allows you to recognize positive and negative reinforcing cycles in yourself. Leaders need to develop their emotional intelligence for themselves, just as much as for the people they lead.

In the next chapter we will look at what an emotionally effective leader looks like in day-to-day life.

Summary

The qualities of effective leadership are well understood. We can all point to experiences we have had being led by others and say whether we feel that was good or bad leadership. But if it's so easy to identify positive leadership behavior, why is great leadership seemingly so rare?

One of the reasons is that leadership doesn't occur in comfortable, low stress, and simple environments. Instead, it is transacted in often frantic, high-paced situations by leaders who are overworked, tired, and frustrated. Leading well is tough.

As we begin our exploration of emotional intelligence, it's important to understand that your EQ doesn't operate on its own. It's influenced by your underlying beliefs. It's also important to understand the role that emotional intelligence plays in the demonstration of the 'technical skills' of leadership.

Additional resources and exercises are available online at http://myeqcoach.com/lgeibook

2

The Emotionally Effective Leader

The emotionally effective leader is one who has a high emotional intelligence quotient. They are able to understand themselves, what they believe, and who they are as a leader. What's more is that they can understand and connect with others. They can empathize, understand, and communicate with the people around them, making them more effective as a leader, while also impacting the effectiveness of those they lead.

Who Is This Emotionally Effective Leader?

Here is an example of what an emotionally effective leader looks like. As you read through, please do keep in mind that emotional intelligence is a complex construct and a great leader adapts their emotional intelligence to the situations they find themselves in. They assess people and situations, so they know what to say, when, and to whom in order to keep people motivated, maintain control over the situation, and ensure the people around them are engaged in the process.

Our emotionally effective leader, who we will call Beth, is self-assured and confident without being overly pushy or arrogant. She recognizes both her leadership strengths and where she has opportunities for growth.

Beth challenges herself to meaningful and ambitious goals – goals that may have nothing to do with promotions or pay increases. These goals might involve achieving a better work-life balance, learning a new skill, or simply developing one or more areas of her leadership. However, these goals do not dominate her behavior or overshadow her sense of living in the moment. Further, she doesn't project her goals or ambitions onto others. Beth recognizes that everyone has their own goals and ambition, and works to understand and support those as well.

Beth has a strong understanding of her emotions and is able to identify in herself what triggers an emotional reaction. She understands how those reactions can color her beliefs, judgments, or actions. When she needs time to think about an issue, to better understand her reactions or impulses, she takes the time to do just that.

She expresses, clearly and consistently, how she feels about a situation or issue. Her body language is congruent with her words so others don't have to guess how she is feeling, what mood she is in, or where she stands on an issue or opportunity. Some of Beth's co-workers say she is easy to read and that you always know where you are with her. She very rarely makes any statement without first considering what she is saying or why she is saying it.

Even in difficult situations, Beth stands up for herself and what she believes in. She takes action as necessary, being appropriately swayed or affected by the well-being of those around her. She doesn't avoid tough decisions, either.

When having a discussion or making a decision, she considers the input of others and factors that into the process, but stands on her own should the need arise. Beth accepts that not every decision she makes will be popular or correct. However, she reflects on each and every decision to determine whether it should have been different and what can be learned. She is self-directed and self-motivated.

Beth works hard to build healthy, mutually beneficial relationships with those around her, both at work and at home. She recognizes the value of relationships, supporting others as needed and accepting support when it is offered. She knows that relationships should be measured by their quality, not their quantity, and has a small, close-knit group of friends who are her confidantes and support system.

She understands that everyone's experience of the world is not the same as her own, and offers support to others, where appropriate, based on that understanding. Beth fully accepts that others may not always be able or willing to do the same for her. Whenever she is confused about another person's words or actions, she takes the time to try and understand what she might be missing, and asks for clarification.

Beth contributes meaningfully to the groups and organizations she is a part of, both inside and outside of work. She acts in a socially responsible way towards others whether they are known to her or not. When circumstances permit, she volunteers her time for a local charity and periodically contributes to causes and organizations she feels strongly about. She acknowledges that while her work with a non-profit group may appear to be a demonstration of her generosity, she receives a great deal of joy and satisfaction in helping others. In general, though, Beth does the socially responsible thing every time an opportunity arises, irrespective of whether someone is watching.

When faced with an emotionally laden problem or challenge, Beth tackles it in an appropriate and timely fashion. She doesn't avoid the tough stuff that comes with being a leader and sees this as a challenging but necessary part of her role.

She understands what parts of the problem, and her perspective on it, can be colored or influenced by her own emotional reactions and experiences, and what parts of the problem are true, tangible facts. She neither fantasizes about overly positive outcomes, nor dramatizes unrealistically negative ones. When possible, she will test theories and hypotheses before taking action to ensure she hasn't missed anything.

After weighing all the options and available information, Beth takes action at an appropriate time, neither moving forward too soon, nor putting it off for too long. When she feels like she may be rushing into a decision too quickly, she will acknowledge it, back off, and consider what is driving her. She rarely makes impulsive decisions.

Beth is open to ideas, suggestions, viewpoints, or perspectives that she may not be aware of, and accepts that other people may see things differently, or better than she does. However, she doesn't shift her stance for the sake of simplicity or in the hope that she might garner more favor. While Beth tends to plan and thoughtfully consider her next move, she understands and enjoys some spontaneity as well.

Beth recognizes the situations that create stress for her and deals with them appropriately. She continues to explore and understand her own emotional triggers and stresses and devises ways to ensure that stress does not color her judgment or cause her to act incongruently with her values and beliefs. Over time, she has developed a range of healthy stress management activities, many of which she integrates into her daily life.

Finally, Beth has a generally positive outlook on life, seeing each day as part of the journey, rather than focusing on any one specific destination. She leads with a sense of positivity and a strong belief that although there are things she might want to change, there are many things for which she is grateful. When she does meet a tough challenge, she knows she can rely on her internal reserves as well as the support and encouragement of others.

Ready to Go?

If the leader that I have described sounds like the kind of leader you would like to be, then you are in the right place. Throughout this book, I will help you explore each one of these areas of emotional intelligence in detail and provide you with the means and tools to create a development plan that will support you in working towards your goals. But before we get the that, there is one more point I'd like to make.

The Knowing-Doing Gap

Before we move on to exploring intelligences, I want to introduce an important concept: the knowing-doing gap. The knowing-doing gap is what holds many leaders back from being effective.

You'll recall that I mentioned, in the last chapter, that I've seen leaders do well at role playing in a classroom, but then fail to implement those skills back in the workplace. That's the knowing-doing gap in action.

To get the results you want and have the impact you seek, you will need to cross the knowing-doing gap. Put more simply, it's not enough to know what you should do. You have to actually do it. This is where you move from emotional intelligence to emotional effectiveness.

We know what an emotionally effective leader looks like. But it will be key to take that knowledge and turn it into action. Chapters 6 and 7 will help you develop a plan to turn your knowledge into action and overcome the knowing-doing gap.

Until then, let's take a deeper look at the elements that contribute to emotional intelligence, emotional effectiveness, and effective leadership.

Summary

If you have ever worked for an emotionally effective leader, you probably saw some elements of his or her behavior in the description above. The truth is that leaders who are highly effective in every area of their emotional intelligence are rare. We all have some work to do on our emotional intelligence in order to reach the very highest levels of emotional effectiveness.

As well, as we will discuss later in this book, just because you can be emotionally effective, doesn't mean you will be. And just because you can be emotionally effective in some areas today, doesn't mean you will be able to maintain those levels of emotional effectiveness every day. Welcome to the complex and sometimes confounding world of emotional intelligence!

Additional resources and exercises are available online at http://myeqcoach.com/lgeibook

Section 1: Homework

Activity 1: Your Leadership Landscape

Your homework for this section includes two activities. The first is a reflective activity called *Your Leadership Landscape*. It's designed to prompt you to think about your current situation. We will draw on this activity later in Chapter 6. You will find the worksheet for this activity in the online resources section.

Your Leadership Landscape is intended for you to take stock of what is happening for you right now in your leadership. Rather than simply completing the activity now, I encourage you spend a few days thinking about the questions. While you may be able to answer some without thinking too hard, others may be worthy of more reflection and consideration.

Here are the seven questions I want you to reflect on and answer before you start the next chapter:

1. What do you like most about your role as a leader?
2. What do you like least about your role as a leader?
3. What are three things that are currently working well for you in your day-to-day leadership?
4. What are three things that you would like to be working better in your day-to-day leadership?
5. Which three relationships in your workplace/

leadership are currently working well for you? Why?

6. Which three relationships in your workplace / leadership are not currently working well for you? Why?

7. If you could improve, influence, or affect one thing about your current leadership landscape what would it be (be detailed)?

The more detailed your answers to these questions, and the more time you take to respond to them, the more useful the activity will be for understanding where you are and how you see yourself as a leader.

You can find the worksheet for this activity on the Resources webpage that accompanies this book: http://myeqcoach.com/lgeibook/

Activity 2: Future You - The Leadership Award

While *Your Leadership Landscape* is designed to help you gauge your current situation, *Future You* is designed to get you thinking about the future of your leadership. This is what I would like you to do:

Imagine that 10 years from now you've won an award for being an outstanding leader. You've been invited to a fancy awards ceremony at the top hotel in town. Many business leaders from across the region will be in attendance, as well as members of your own team, your own manager and the CEO of your organization. They are all looking forward to celebrating your amazing achievement with you.

As part of the awards ceremony you've been asked to provide an acceptance speech, and conference organizers have given you some specific requests. In addition to telling those at the gala dinner about your leadership journey, they want you to also share your personal Top Five Leadership Practices. These practices are the things that you did every day, or that you wove consistently into your leadership, that you felt had the most impact.

For example, it may be that you never shied away from a difficult decision, or that you always canvassed the opinion of everyone in your group before making a tough choice. Keep in mind that your team and your manager will be present in the audience so you can only tell the attendees about things you actually did, not about things you would have liked to do.

With this future in mind, what leadership practices would you give that are representative of the great leader that you currently are or the leader that you are working to be. Make a list of all of those practices, some of which you may already be doing, and choose the 5 that you feel are the most important.

As with *Your Leadership Landscape*, you will find a worksheet for *Future You* on the Resources webpage - http://myeqcoach.com/lgeibook/.

It is important that you complete this activity as we will be referring to it later in the book.

With both *Your Leadership Landscape* and *Future You*, if you have any questions or comments, please remember to drop me a line at info@myeqcoach.com and I will be happy to help out.

Additional resources and exercises are available
online at http://myeqcoach.com/lgeibook

Section 2

Understanding Emotional Intelligence

3

Exploring Intelligences

In the last chapter, we investigated what an emotionally effective leader looks like on a day-to-day basis. But how did we arrive at being able to describe this thing called emotional intelligence in such a way? And, aren't we just describing human behavior?

Well, the answer to that question is yes, but having a framework or structure to describe this behavior is a key element in developing it. You have to name something in order to go to work on it.

In this chapter, we will look at the history of emotional intelligence study and understand how it has come to been understood as such an important aspect of leadership. I will take you through an exploration of your leadership development priorities, and explain the difference between EI and EQ.

What Is Intelligence?

Intelligence is defined as the ability to acquire and apply knowledge and skills. When we talk about intelligence, most people are familiar with cognitive intelligence, which we measure through tests of intelligence quotient (IQ). Although IQ is the most well-known intelligence, there are many other types of intelligence to be aware of.

As with most everything in the realm of psychology, there is a scientific definition and an everyday definition, the latter of which people tend to be more familiar with. If you ask most people about their definition of cognitive intelligence, for example, they'll say it has to do with math and/or language, and they would be correct. But there is more to it than that. Let me show you what I mean.

Cognitive Intelligence

Cognitive intelligence is actually a highly complex construct. In 1993, J.B. Carroll developed a model of cognitive intelligence that starts with general intelligence (g). From there, Carroll broke cognitive intelligence down into eight broad abilities, such as Crystallised Intelligence, Broad Auditory Perception, and Processing Speed. By breaking cognitive intelligence down in this way, we can assess, measure, and potentially improve specific areas of someone's cognitive intelligence. For example, you might decide to undertake activities that would increase your Processing Speed or your General Memory and Learning.

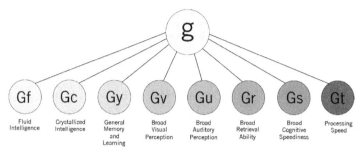

J.B. Carroll (1993). *Human cognitive abilities: A survey of factor-analytic studies*, Cambridge University Press, New York, NY, USA

Now you might be thinking, "I thought this was a book about emotional intelligence. Why is he telling me about cognitive intelligence?" The reason we discuss this model, though, is to demonstrate that in order to understand constructs like intelligence, it's useful to have conceptual models that break down and identify the elements of that type of intelligence. And that broad definitions, while easy to remember, are not actually that useful if you want to take action or address something more specifically. As you'll see later, we use a similar approach to understanding emotional intelligence.

Now, while most people are familiar with cognitive intelligence, it's worth noting that there are many other accepted types of intelligence as well.

Types of Intelligence

In 1983, Howard Gardner conceptualized and defined nine different types of intelligence. In his book, *Frames of Mind: The Theory of Multiple Intelligences*, he suggests that people have a range of distinct abilities and intelligences that influence who they are and what they are good at in different ways. For example, you might know someone who seems to be naturally gifted at learning music or playing an instrument. They may be *musically intelligent*. In other words, they are adept at hearing pitch, tone, and timbre, and may also have a natural ability to keep a rhythm. They may also have a high level of *kinesthetic intelligence*, which is what makes it possible for them to control their movements to play an instrument.

1 **Naturalist Intelligence (Nature Smart)**
Sensitivity and ability to understand the natural world.

2 **Linguistic Intelligence (Word Smart)**
Ability to understand complex words, languages, and connections.

3 **Existential Intelligence**
Connecting to the larger questions of humanity, philosophy, etc.

4 **Spatial Intelligence (Picture Smart)**
Ability to see things in 3-dimensions, understand spatial relatedness. Sometimes referred to as spatial reasoning.

5 **Logical-Mathematical Intelligence (Number Smart)**
Ability to work with numbers, make numerical connections, etc.

6 **Bodily-Kiensthetic Intelligence (Body Smart)**
Ability to use the body for activities or tasks.

7 **Musical Intelligence (Music Smart)**
Ability to hear pitch, tone, timbre, etc.

8 **Intra-personal Intelligence (Self Smart)**
Ability to understand self, and use that information in a meaningful and useful way.

9 **Interpersonal Intelligence (People Smart**
Ability to make connections with others, understand emotional information and communicate effectively in a verbal and non-verbal way.

Based on information from *Frames of Mind: The Theory of Multiple Intelligences* - Garnder, 1983

Similarly, you might know someone who is particularly artistic or creative. They may possess a higher level of *spatial intelligence*, which is an ability to understand and conceptualize objects in three dimensions, and, again, a higher level of *kinesthetic intelligence*, which allows them to translate ideas into physical pieces of art.

Two of the intelligences that Gardner identified, *intrapersonal intelligence* and *interpersonal intelligence*, relate to emotional intelligence. According to Gardner, intrapersonal intelligence is the ability to understand oneself and use that information in a meaningful way, including a willingness to be self-reflective and an openness to understanding and learning about oneself. Interpersonal intelligence, then, is the ability to make connections with others and to understand emotional information.

Knowing that there are different kinds of 'smart' enables us, as people, to acknowledge, understand, appreciate, and value the different talents and skills that each person brings to the table. Just because someone is not good at math or they don't have good interpersonal skills doesn't mean they're not intelligent.

That said, in the context of our discussion of leadership, these things do matter. While we may have been able to use our spatial or kinesthetic intelligence to reach our goals as individual contributors or subject matter experts, as a leader we are most focused on the intrapersonal and interpersonal intelligences.

If you recall the *Good Leader, Bad Leader* exercise from Chapter 1, when it comes to evaluating effective leadership behavior, it is primarily the intrapersonal and interpersonal intelligences that have the greatest impact on leadership ability. As these are directly related to emotional intelligence, let's take a look at this concept now.

Defining Emotional Intelligence

Although not included in Gardner's multiple intelligences under that name, emotional intelligence is based on two of Gardner's categories: interpersonal and intrapersonal intelligences. Throughout this book, we will refer to these, together, as emotional intelligence.

When defining and examining emotional intelligence, we deal with five domains of understanding:

- How we see ourselves
- How we express ourselves
- How we build and maintain relationships with others
- How we understand our environment and make decisions
- How we deal with stressful or difficult situations

Similar to the way we defined the broad areas of ability in cognitive intelligence, this five-domain model is the beginning of our journey into understanding emotional intelligence as a construct. That's great, but how did we get here in the first place?

A Brief History of Emotional Intelligence

The first references to emotional intelligence can be traced back to Ancient Greek philosophy. However, in modern times it was Charles Darwin's writings on the expression of emotion in humans and animals that first acknowledged the idea that there may be more to intelligence and success than simply being 'smart.'

Darwin noted that humans and animals interact with each other using emotional information, through body language, facial expressions, tone, and, in humans, words. Darwin recognized that understanding these interactions was an important part of success in social functioning.

In 1920, Edward Thorndike devised the principal of *social intelligence*, or a person's ability to understand people and cooperate with them. Fast-forward to 1983 when Gardner developed the theory of multiple intelligences.

At each step in this process, the conceptualization of the construct became clearer. In 1990, two researchers, Peter Salovey and John D. Mayer wrote a paper called 'Emotional Intelligence. Imagination, Cognition, and Personality' that introduced the term and the modern definition of emotional intelligence.

The exploration and understanding of emotional and social intelligence, in recent years, has become popular among psychologists and business people alike. In 1996, Daniel Goleman published his seminal book, *Emotional Intelligence: Why It Can Matter More than IQ*. This book, which I highly recommend you read, essentially brought emotional intelligence into the broader public understanding.

Goleman's book, which drew from much of the previous work on emotional intelligence, put the construct and principles of emotional intelligence into an easily understandable format. His real-world examples struck a chord with leaders who, at the time, were often focusing solely on those technical skills I referred to in Chapter 1.

In 1997, Reuven Bar-On, a South African researcher and psychologist, published *The Bar-On EQ-i™ Technical Manual*, which detailed his model of emotional intelligence. This extremely useful, and easy-to-understand model was the culmination of many years of research and investigation into the concepts of emotional intelligence. Bar-On's model specifically focused on the traits of emotional intelligence.

To accompany the model, he created a self-assessment tool and a multi-rater, 360-degree feedback tool to help people measure their emotional intelligence traits across the different competencies. In the first decade of the 21st Century, Bar-On's model of emotional intelligence became one of the most popular and widely accepted models of emotional intelligence in existence.

In 2011, Bar-On worked with a North American clinical assessment provider, Multi-Health Systems, to update the original model and released it as *EQ-i 2.0*, a revised model of emotional intelligence. This is the model we will refer to and use throughout this book.

It's worth noting that there are many brilliant scientists and researchers who have contributed to the development of emotional intelligence over the past century and a half. Although I haven't mentioned each individual here, let us recognize that many have contributed to the models and research we currently use to assess and define emotional intelligence.

The EQ-i 2.0 Model of Emotional Intelligence

The EQ-i 2.0 Model of Emotional Intelligence (shown on the next page), developed by Bar-On and updated with Multi-Health Systems, uses a 1-5-15 factor model. The 1 is the construct of emotional intelligence: the button in the center. The large pie slices that divide the model are the 5 composite scales, each referring to a broad area of emotional intelligence. The smaller words in the middle ring represent the 15 specific competencies of emotional intelligence, or what we call subscales. There are three subscales in each of the composite scales. It is primarily through these 15 subscales that we assess and understand EQ development.

The next chapter will delve deeper into this model. For now, keep this broad explanation in mind.

EI or EQ?

Although the terms EI and EQ are often easily confused, the main difference is that EI is what emotional intelligence is, and your EQ is how much EI you have.

EI, or emotional intelligence, is the term we use to describe the construct of emotional intelligence. If we go back to our discussion of cognitive intelligence and apply the same rule, we would be referring to cognitive intelligence as CI. EQ, or emotional quotient, then, is the term we use to refer to the amount of EI that person has. Similarly, when we measure cognitive intelligence, or CI, we do so using a construct called intelligence quotient or IQ.

While this may seem like a small and perhaps irrelevant detail, it's worth keeping in mind as we go through this book and when you do additional reading on emotional intelligence. The bottom line is that many people use EI and EQ to refer to the same thing, sometimes in the same passage or paragraph. While this may not be 100% technically accurate, as long as you are aware of what is being referred to it doesn't much matter.

Flavor of The Month?

When I meet with leadership groups about emotional intelligence, most people are not only interested but fascinated by the idea that we have been able to identify these key skills and attributes of effective leadership. However, there are some who criticize emotional intelligence for being a fad or the flavor-of-the-month.

However, if you wanted to level such a criticism at emotional intelligence, you would more likely have to call it the flavor-of-the-*century*. According to Fortune Magazine (1999), "Business leaders are no longer being defined by their IQs or even their technical skills. It is their emotional intelligence that makes the difference. It is rarely for the lack of smarts or vision. Most unsuccessful leaders stumble because of one simple, fatal shortcoming. The failure is one of emotional strength."

You might be forgiven for thinking that this was a recent quote, but in fact it was published in Fortune Magazine more than 16 years ago. It holds true even today, as a lack of emotional strength is still one of the most common things holding leaders back.

Summary

The idea that there are multiple intelligences has been around for a very long time and through the hard work and dedication of many skilled and gifted researchers we are now able to understand emotional intelligence in a meaningful way.

It's good to know that emotional intelligence is not a fad or horoscope. This is a serious, scientifically researched construct. Knowing how we classify EQ, and using a model to understand the construct is hugely important. In the next chapter, we will dig into the EQ-i Model of Emotional Intelligence in more detail.

Additional resources and exercises are available online at http://myeqcoach.com/lgeibook

4

Understanding the EQ-i Model of Emotional Intelligence

At the end of the last chapter I showed you the EQ-i model. It's this model that we will use as the platform for your ongoing EQ development. In order to do that, we need to understand the various components of the model and how they all fit together.

We also need to understand the relationship between the different parts of the model, but we will cover that in the next chapter. I am excited to share the model with you, so let's get started.

The EQ-i 2.0 Model

As I mentioned briefly in the previous chapter, models of emotional intelligence allow us to understand and develop emotional competencies in a clear and meaningful way.

The EQ-i 2.0 Model of Emotional Intelligence, or as we will refer to it from now on, the EQ-i model, is divided up into five broad areas, or composite scales, of emotional intelligence. They are:

- **Self-Perception**, which is concerned with the internal functions of how we see and understand ourselves. The Self Perception Composite's subscales are:
    - Self-Regard
    - Self-Actualization
    - Emotional Self-Awareness

- **Self-Expression**, which connects with the way we express thoughts and emotions in our daily lives. The three subscales are:
  - Emotional Expression
  - Assertiveness
  - Independence
- **Interpersonal**, which relates to how well we manage and maintain relationships with other people, as well as our role in the groups that we are a part of and our broader social context. The subscales in this composite are:
  - Interpersonal Relationships
  - Empathy
  - Social Responsibility
- **Decision Making**, which involves how we make decisions and interact with our world. The three subscales here are:
  - Problem-Solving
  - Reality Testing
  - Impulse Control
- **Stress Management**, which deals with how we understand, process, and react to difficult or stressful situations. The three subscales are:
  - Flexibility
  - Stress Tolerance
  - Optimism

Although the composite scales provide a way of grouping together the individual subscales in the most relevant way, the subscales are what we are most interested in when it comes to understanding and developing our emotional intelligence. Let's take a look at each composite in more detail to better understand the behaviors, characteristics, and actions, associated with each.

The Self-Perception Composite

Self-perception is the way we understand ourselves in relation to the world. It includes how we see ourselves, the goals we set, and how aware we are of our emotions and reactions.

Self-Regard

Self-Regard is the way that we see ourselves as a whole person. It is the extent to which we respect ourselves while understanding and accepting both strengths and weaknesses. Self-Regard is often associated with feelings of inner strength and self-confidence.

Individuals with a high level Self-Regard may come across as very confident and sure of themselves. They may feel like they rarely make mistakes and that their ideas or opinions are generally correct or best. In contrast, people with a low level of Self-Regard may come across as uncertain or insecure. They may doubt their abilities and take failures, or perceived failures, very hard. They may indulge in frequent negative self-talk.

As you can imagine, in a leadership role it is important to have a certain level of confidence in your ability and inner strength, but a well-developed sense of Self-Regard also acknowledges that we all have areas to develop and grow.

Self-Actualization

Self-Actualization refers to the extent to which a person sets and works towards meaningful goals. It includes the willingness to persistently try to improve oneself and engage in the pursuit of personally relevant and meaningful objectives that lead to a rich and enjoyable life.

Generally speaking, human beings are goal-oriented individuals and while goals may differ greatly from person to person, the desire to set and achieve goals is a common trait.

It might seem like having a very high level of Self-Actualization would be a good thing, and it definitely can be, however we need to be careful that we don't project our levels of ambition and goal-orientation onto other people, or judge their levels of goal-setting negatively if they aren't in line with own standards of ambition.

Emotional Self-Awareness

Emotional Self-Awareness refers to our ability and willingness to examine and understand our own emotional reactions. This includes the ability to differentiate between subtleties in our emotions while understanding their cause and the impact they have on our thoughts and actions.

As an example, while it's a totally acceptable human reaction to be angry at something, an emotionally self-aware person knows and understands what they are angry about and why they feel this way. They can also differentiate which parts of their reaction relate to the current situation, as opposed to prior experiences.

Individuals with a low level of Emotional Self-Awareness tend to not think through situations to better understand their reactions, and may have a limited vocabulary when it comes to expressing their emotions. They may react to a situation, or other people, in a certain way without really understanding why.

In contrast, somebody with a very high level of emotional self-awareness will take considerable time and energy to better understand their emotional reaction to a situation. Of course, neither of these extremes are useful or necessarily appropriate, so the key will be to find a balance between a disinterest in emotions and an almost obsessive level of self-reflection.

The Self-Expression Composite

Self-Expression is the way in which we express ourselves to the world. It involves the ways we communicate our emotions and feelings, how we describe our thoughts, feelings, and beliefs, and to what extent we are comfortable working and being on our own.

Emotional Expression

If Emotional Self-Awareness is our ability to accurately understand our emotional reactions and states, Emotional Expression is our ability to communicate those emotions accurately and clearly to another person. When we think about Emotional Expression, we think about the entire range of human communication, including body language, facial expressions, tone, and the words we choose to use.

You've probably met people who have a very high level of Emotional Expression. They are the ones who don't keep you guessing about how they're feeling or what they are thinking. You may even say that they wear their heart on their sleeve.

You may also know people with a lower level of Emotional Expression, who are hard to read, and who seem incongruent with the words they speak and the tone or body language they display. For many people, this can be very unsettling, so a quality leader must be able to demonstrate strong levels of Emotional Expression. Followers love a leader they can understand, so the clearer you can be about your message and the more congruently you can communicate that message, the more likely followers will be to believe it.

Assertiveness

Assertiveness refers to our ability to openly communicate our thoughts, beliefs and feelings. Very high levels of Assertiveness can sometimes be associated with strong or pushy people. It's important to know, however, that Assertiveness is not arrogance. One of the key descriptors for Assertiveness is that it relates to how well we assert ourselves in a socially acceptable and non-offensive way. As with all of the other subscales, leaders need to strike a balance between being appropriately Assertive and sufficiently collaborative in their day-to-day activities.

Very Assertive leaders may push their opinions and perspectives on others, sometimes at the expense of the rest of the team. But on the flip side of the equation, followers value a leader who has opinions and is willing to stand up for what they believe in. As you've probably guessed by now, when it comes to emotional intelligence and leadership, there tends to be a fine balance between too much and not enough.

Independence

Independence is our ability to be self-directed and free from emotional dependency on others. For independent leaders, decision making, planning, and daily tasks can be completed autonomously. In the realm of emotional intelligence, we are referring to an ability to work alone and manage emotional concerns and issues without disrupting others or needing excessive emotional support.

For a leader to be effective, they need to be close enough, on an interpersonal level, to the people that they lead, but far enough away that they are able to make tough decisions. Leaders with a low level of Independence will tend to care too much about what other people think of their actions and as result, may shy away from decisions that will impact people in the group. Conversely, leaders with a very high level of Independence may not connect sufficiently with the people they lead, and may operate too independently of the group.

The Interpersonal Composite

The Interpersonal Composite examines how we relate to other people in our lives. This includes how we manage relationships with other people, how we show empathy and care for others, and how concerned we are with the people around us in our broader social context.

Interpersonal Relationships

The Interpersonal Relationships subscale deals with our ability to establish and maintain meaningful relationships with other people. This involves the extent to which we rely on others, how well we manage compromise, and how satisfying we find the relationships we are in. Much of this is strongly correlated to our ability to build trust and compassion with the people around us.

For some people, Interpersonal Relationships are an incredibly important and significant part of their life, while others may appear not to appreciate these relationships quite so much. While some have large groups of friends, others tend to keep a smaller circle or prefer to spend time alone. However, there is a clear distinction in the context of Interpersonal Relationships that the concern is about the quality of the relationships rather than the quantity, so even people who spend time in smaller groups can have a high Interpersonal Relationships quotient.

People with strong Interpersonal Relationships will place value on what it means to be able to connect with and work with other people. They will likely seek to establish deep and trusting relationships with others and will find it easy to meet people and make friends. They will also recognize that these interpersonal relationships are a source of support and help in difficult times.

People with a lower level of Interpersonal Relationships may find it harder to make new friends and may see the social relationships they have as less necessary. However, it does not mean that they don't like other people or don't want to have relationships.

One of the challenges that leaders face is that they may want to create strong interpersonal bonds with the people they lead. While this has its upsides, it is important to build consistent bonds across the whole team, so as not to show favorites or be exclusionary to anyone.

Empathy

Empathy is our ability to recognize, understand and appreciate how others feel. This includes being able to understand those feelings and behaving in a way that is respectful to them.

Daniel Goleman has said that Empathy is the single most important emotional intelligence skill a leader can have. This makes sense when you think about it. If a leader is unable or reluctant to empathize with another person, what chance do they have in understanding where they are coming from?

Empathy should not be confused with sympathy. Sympathy is when you feel *sorry, or bad, for* someone. Conversely, Empathy is when you can actually understand and *feel with* them through the experience. Empathy allows you to explore, on a deeper level, what the other person is experiencing, as opposed to being an observer or bystander.

Of course, as with any part of emotional intelligence, you can have too much Empathy. At the end of the day, the work needs to get done and people come to work to do a job. An effective leader must strike a balance between acknowledging and accommodating the needs of the individuals in their team and ensuring that the goals and objectives of the team are met.

Social Responsibility

Social Responsibility, in this context, is related to our willingness to be a part of social groups and recognize that we are part of a larger whole in terms of our community, our country, and humanity. It involves acting responsibly, being conscious of societal needs, and showing concern for our community.

We might measure Social Responsibility by looking at the ways in which people contribute their time or money to meaningful causes, but it isn't just about actions; it is also about mindset and perspective. If we are able to see the broader reach and impact of our behaviors and actions, we may not behave a certain way or take those actions in the first place.

Now, if you're wondering why Social Responsibility is part of emotional intelligence, consider that emotional intelligence is about emotional and social skills. So, how we fit into the big picture socially is important. From a leadership perspective, those with a higher-level of Social Responsibility may act in environmentally responsible ways and encourage their team to do the same. Those with a lower level of Social Responsibility may feel that small changes make no difference and so pay less attention to the environmental impact their work has.

The Decision Making Composite

The Decision Making Composite deals with how we go about the daily tasks of life, how we choose to handle situations, which activities we choose to engage in, and how well we control the impulses we have.

People make hundreds, if not thousands, of decisions every day. Some of these decisions are small and made without any serious attention, like whether to drink a glass of water or not. Some are much larger and complex, and require substantial thought and consideration.

By its very nature, leadership requires quite a lot of decision making, so a high score in these competencies will greatly benefit anyone in a leadership position. However, most leaders have never trained their decision-making capacity, and so have never improved their ability to think through and consider options and come to the best conclusions.

Problem Solving

In the context of emotional intelligence, Problem Solving refers to our ability to solve emotionally laden or emotionally challenging problems, as opposed to solving logistical or technical problems, although it is sometimes difficult to tell them apart!

Additionally, the Problem Solving competency is based on how well we understand the impact emotions have on our decisions. It comes down to being able to manage the emotions involved with certain decisions, understanding who might be affected by these decisions, and considering what the consequences might be.

Some examples include dealing with a staff member's performance issue or deciding who we must lay off because of budgetary constraints. Both of these decisions involve emotion – both yours and your employees' – and ignoring or denying that emotion is an impediment to a balanced decision-making process.

Leaders who have a strong Problem Solving competency will tend to tackle problems head-on and analyze the issue or situation from a variety of angles. They will carefully consider the impact of their options, but they won't delay acting for too long. In fact, one of the signs of a leader who struggles with Problem Solving is that they will put off making a decision, while some even deny the existence of issues in the first place.

Reality Testing

Reality Testing refers to our ability to see things objectively and as they really are. Most people have a set of biases that impact the way they see the world and how they relate to others. Having a strong Reality Testing competency includes being able to remove these biases, instead of fantasizing or catastrophizing about potential outcomes.

Leaders with a strong sense of Reality Testing will go to great lengths to understand what is going on in a specific situation. This may often involve collecting information and evidence and asking multiple people for their perspectives. They understand where their biases lie and how they might be able to transcend these biases in order to understand the situation more objectively.

There is a risk, however, that data collection may go on too long, or biases may prevail, inhibiting the leader's decision-making capacity. Paralysis-by-analysis can sometimes mean that leaders will avoid tough decisions because they always believe there is more information that should be considered.

Impulse Control

Impulse Control, when it comes to emotional intelligence, it a person's ability to resist impulsive and tempting behaviors and decisions, especially when it comes to emotionally-charged situations. When Impulse Control is low, people have a difficult time refraining from doing or saying something inappropriate or making the wrong decision.

You would be amazed at the number of leaders who struggle with Impulse Control. Most commonly, this presents itself when a leader interrupts others during conversations, makes hasty decisions, or talks too much.

One of the most common pieces of feedback we see in multi-rater or 360° feedback is that followers think their leaders talk too much and don't listen. However, having too high a level of Impulse Control doesn't work either. This is the domain of talking oneself out of saying or doing something by leaving too much time for rationalization.

The Stress Management Composite

Stress Management refers to the ways in which we manage stress within ourselves, as well as how we express our stress to others. It involves being able to adapt to difficult situations, handling stressful encounters positively, and the extent to which we have a generally positive outlook on life.

Flexibility

Flexibility is our ability and willingness to see things from different perspectives – to be open to new ideas or ways of doing things and to easily adapt our beliefs. It involves adapting our emotions, thoughts, and behaviors to unfamiliar and unpredictable circumstances, especially those that might cause stress.

People with lower levels of Flexibility might be described as stubborn and somewhat difficult. They may suffer from higher levels of stress because they need or want situations to always be familiar to them.

On the other hand, a high level of Flexibility also has its downsides. While followers like leaders who are open to new ideas and ways of doing things, they also want to know that once decisions have been made, the leader will not flip-flop or change their mind unless there is good reason to do so.

Leaders with an optimal level of Flexibility are able to adapt and thrive in unfamiliar situations, but never lose sight of their self and their own emotions, thoughts, and behaviors.

Stress Tolerance

Stress Tolerance is the way we manage and deal with stressful situations. It involves the ability to cope with the situation and manage stress levels, as well as the way we express that stress. A key element to stress tolerance is the extent to which we believe we can positively influence situations.

People with lower levels of Stress Tolerance may become easily flustered when things get difficult and revert to traditional ways of problem solving and management. They often allow their stress levels to be seen and to affect those around them. Low Stress Tolerance is also associated with feelings of being unable to affect or change the situation.

On the other end of the scale, you might think there could be nothing bad about a leader with a very high level of Stress Tolerance, however if the leader's Stress Tolerance is much higher than the people they lead, this can cause problems. In situations like this, the leader may not understand the impact stressful situation might have on the team, and the team may see the leader as too laid back or uncaring. This incongruence of Stress Tolerance could greatly affect the trust and empathy a team has in their leader.

Optimism

As it suggests, Optimism is how positively one views life in general. It involves feelings of hopefulness and resilience in the face of challenges.

High levels of Optimism are associated with a bright, cheery, and positive outlook. In general, the more the better, but just as with Stress Tolerance, too much can affect the way in which leaders take problems seriously and the way their positive attitude is interpreted by people around them. There are many situations in which it is inappropriate to be overly cheerful.

On the other hand, lower levels of Optimism often result in negative thoughts and little hope for the future. Those with low Optimism can negatively affect the overall morale of the team and leaders who don't display a positive outlook may not inspire others.

It makes sense that Optimism would be in the Stress Management composite, as it is in stressful situations that we are required to summon our inner strength and Optimism as a mechanism for working through them.

As you can see, the EQ-i model is a comprehensive way of understand emotional intelligence. That's one of the reasons I think it's the best model of emotional and social competence we have today. By breaking the EQ construct out into this level of detail, we can easily identify and go to work on the elements that will have the most impact on our leadership. With that in mind, lets dig a little further into how it can help in both professional and personal development.

How The EQ-i Model Helps

Using a model to understand emotional intelligence helps in a number of ways. The first, and perhaps most significant, is that by naming something, you can start to work on it. Not only that, but once it is explained and defined, you can understand its importance, why you should work on it, and the ways in which you display it to others.

The EQ-i model provides a structure and platform for developing and improving your overall EQ. By first assessing yourself and analyzing the results, you can select specific subscales to work on, and over time, you can develop your emotional intelligence.

For example, if I were to suggest that you should be more reflective when making decisions, you would need to analyze that statement further before coming to realize that I am referring to Impulse Control. And, by having a definition for Impulse Control and understanding both of the low and high ends of that subscale, you can develop strategies for improving that aspect of your emotional intelligence.

By naming subscales, you can also see where others demonstrate their emotional intelligence. Through observing and listening when others act and speak, you can see how they express their emotions and how you might emulate them.

For example, you might observe someone and admire the way they demonstrate Empathy in interactions with you or another team member. Not only can you recognize this, but you can start to also act this way when you interact with others. Similarly, you might listen to one of your peers passionately explain why they feel a certain way about project and identify their high level of Emotional Expression. Then, you can pick up on subtle ways they express themselves effectively.

Of course, the same applies to how and when people display aspects they could improve on. You can identify when someone is acting with a lower emotional intelligence. Identifying both good and bad examples of emotional intelligence in others can be a powerful learning tool as it helps you to experience emotional intelligence in action.

Always keep in mind, though, that your judgments of emotional intelligence in others will depend on your own EI. For example, just because you think that someone is acting assertively doesn't mean they are. Your *perception* of their actions and your *interpretation* of assertiveness are what will impact your understanding of their behavior.

A third benefit of understanding the EQ-i model is that you can begin to name your own behavior as you reflect on your day-to-day life. You can recognize how you are and start to understand how and why others see you as they do.

For example, you might decide after the meeting that you should've said something. Because you know that speaking up in meeting's is a function of your Assertiveness, you can analyze the conditions for Assertiveness and understand the underlying causes for why you didn't speak up and ways you might work to improve.

Summary

In this chapter we examined and explained the EQ-i model and each of the composites and their subscales. We looked at how Self-Perception affects the ways

87

we understand ourselves and our emotions and how Self-Expression relates to how we demonstrate and communicate those emotions.

Then, we looked at how the Interpersonal subscales affect the ways we build relationships and interact with others, while the Decision Making composite affects our impulses and problem solving. We examined the ways in which Stress Management relates to our general outlook on life and the ways in which we adapt and deal with difficult situations.

Finally, we took a quick look at how the EQ-i Model of Emotional Intelligence can help us assess ourselves, reflect on our behavior, respond to others' behavior, and recognize emotionally intelligent behavior in others.

In the coming chapters, we will take a deeper look at how the subscales work together and the importance of balancing them to better relate to others, understand ourselves, and manage our environment. Then we'll look at how we can develop a more formal plan for improving and building our own emotional intelligence.

Additional resources and exercises are available online at http://myeqcoach.com/lgeibook

5

EQ in Balance

Balancing our emotional intelligences, or rather, the subscales of our EI, requires us to understand how each subscale plays into the next. For example, how our Self-Regard affects our Emotional Expression, or how our Empathy affects our Impulse Control.

In examining this balance, we will begin by looking at what I call the dark side of strengths. Or, how having too high of any competency as compared to the others can negatively impact your effectiveness as a leader. We touched on this a bit in the previous chapter, but now we'll take a look at it in more depth.

Following that, we will examine the key subscale balances that you will need to have in check to be an effective leader. Emotional well-being is key to effectiveness as a leader, so we will look at which subscales can contribute to our well-being, and how emotional well-being impacts leadership effectiveness.

The Dark Side of Strengths

You will recall from the previous chapter that when discussing the subscales of the EQ-i model, I presented examples both of how too low a level can be bad, and of how very high levels of a competency can create challenges. This is particularly the case when two complementary subscales are both at a high level and there is nothing to balance it out. This is what we call the dark side: when one (or more) aspect gets out of control or reaches such a high level that it starts negatively affecting the leader's effectiveness. The dark side of strengths is an important consideration as you reflect on your own emotional intelligence and create a plan for improving it.

Let me give you an example. Imagine a leader, Adam, who is highly assertive. As we know from the discussion in the last chapter, his Assertiveness is the way he communicates his feelings and beliefs, and how strongly he defends his rights and values. Having a high level of Assertiveness can be good, but too high a level can lead to him being unaware of how strongly he defends or communicates. So, he may not realize or recognize the situations in which his high level of Assertiveness can create problems.

Now consider that Adam also has a very high level of Self-Regard. You will recall that leaders with high Self-Regard are sure of themselves and come across as confident. However, with too much Self-Regard, Adam may put himself above others and display behaviors that make people feel as though they are lesser.

When you combine these two characteristics, you have a leader who is very sure of themselves and very confident in their thoughts and beliefs, but who is also strong when it comes to asserting those thoughts and behaviors onto others. As you can imagine, this pairing can create challenges for the leader and those they lead.

When Adam puts himself above others and asserts his thoughts and beliefs very strongly, he begins to display authoritarian behaviors. Rather than taking the time to consider others, he is too busy believing in himself. Rather than accepting others' thoughts and beliefs, he begins to see his own ideas as the most important and pushes his ideas onto the people around him, thereby undermining others' contributions.

The combination of high Self-Regard and Assertiveness is not uncommon, especially in business leaders, so you may well know someone like this. In many ways, having high scores in each subscale can be ideal, as that means we understand ourselves and others, and we can handle most anything that comes to us. However, when only a few competencies score high, especially those that complement each other in this way, the imbalance can cause problems. So you can see that while Adam has high levels of emotional intelligence in a variety of areas, he may not be getting the results he's looking for and does not see how he is impacting others.

Now, we never encourage leaders to reduce or depress their level of emotional intelligence on a given subscale. For example, we would never encourage a leader to try to be less assertive. Instead, what we do is encourage that leader to develop subscales that can balance out their Assertiveness. In this case, the first and most obvious choice would be to help them develop a stronger sense of Empathy. We'll look at this in more detail later in the chapter.

Balance in Action

Ideally, all 15 subscales in your EQ profile would be balanced with all of the others. When we talk about balance, we are referring to developing your subscales to the point where they are somewhat equal or even. In the previous example, that would mean developing Adam's Empathy to approximately the same level as his Assertiveness and Self-Regard, so as to counteract the negative effects of these two competencies.

The assessment tools I use in my work with leaders score each subscale with a numerical value, so we can compare levels of each competency more easily. For example, we score the normal range of emotional intelligence as being between 90 and 110 points on a scale that runs from roughly 60 to 130. Each of the subscales is scored on that scale, as well. So, for example, a leader might have a score of 120 for Assertiveness, and 103 for Empathy. So, we would say they are not in balance. Typically, the cut-off point for balance is when two subscales differ by 10 points or more.

By understanding where you have an imbalance, you can begin to further explore where you might want to start your emotional intelligence development.

It's worth mentioning at this point that in all the assessments I have delivered over the past decade, I have never seen an EI profile that was 100% in balance.

It is quite normal for there to be differences between your subscales. Generally, people have a preference or higher quotient in one composite over the others, or one that is weaker than the others. This doesn't mean we are tyrants or out of control in any way. It simply points to areas in which we need improvement and provides a guide toward where to start with our development plan. Primarily, problems only arise when a few are extremely out of balance or when certain pairings are imbalanced.

This concept of balance is absolutely integral to your understanding of emotional intelligence, so to further illustrate this point let's take a look at a couple common examples of balance and imbalance in emotional intelligence.

Assertiveness-Empathy Imbalance

We will start by looking at the same example I provided earlier: an imbalance between Assertiveness and Empathy. On the one hand we have a leader with a high level of Assertiveness and a lower level of Empathy. As we discussed, they may run into challenges because they don't sufficiently consider or appreciate other people's perspectives or positions in relation to an issue or challenge. This higher level of Assertiveness and lower level of Empathy can result in a leader who is pushy or arrogant.

But let's consider this subscale imbalance in the opposite direction. A leader who has a much higher level of Empathy and a lower level of Assertiveness can face difficulties as well. Because they have a high Empathy quotient, they likely take other people's positions and perspectives much too seriously and perhaps let that impact their decision making.

Often, leaders with high Empathy will allow their concern for others to interfere with their decisions or actions to the detriment of the team. Now add in that they have a low level of Assertiveness, and you have a leader who may let others walk all over them. As we know, the role of a leader is to ensure the work gets done and the group meets its goals. If the leader is too empathetic and not assertive enough, leaders may either sacrifice the team goals in favor of the needs of one individual or they end up not being able to delegate and take on too many tasks because they are too worried about negatively affecting anyone else on the team.

In the short term, there may not be a noticeable effect, because there are times when one person needs special treatment or consideration or the leader can handle a few extra tasks. However, in the long run, this imbalance can have far-reaching effects, such as a team culture where people take advantage of the good nature of the leader, or where work isn't completed because the leader accommodates team members' needs and desires too much.

When Assertiveness and Empathy Are Balanced

When Assertiveness and Empathy are in balance, a leader will be able to take the time to appreciate where others stand on an issue. They have the capacity to listen and take into consideration the ideas and feelings of the people they work with. They can value and listen to the opinions and perspectives of others as they relate to decisions, while also considering a decision's impact on other individuals or the team as a whole.

A leader who has a balance between Empathy and Assertiveness will be able to understand why the team dislikes a decision that was made, or why they opt to support one idea over another. This aids in overall decision making as well.

At the same time, though, this leader won't allow the whims and reactions of an individual dictate the whole team's direction. They will consider these ideas, but will always make decisions that are best for the team, or that the majority of the team supports. They hold their own opinions in regard, as well as those of the team, thereby allowing them to take advantage of their own expertise and decision making ability.

A leader that balances Empathy and Assertiveness knows when they have to make a hard decision and stands by that decision despite any negative reactions. At the same time, however, the leader can fully understand and empathize with those who were negatively affected. In doing this, they can show their care for those individuals and offer support to manage the tough decision.

This means the leader can ensure things get done and uphold the goals of the team, but can also understand where individuals on the team are coming from and provide additional encouragement. This way, the team achieves its goals, and the individuals on the team know their leader is there for them and that they did not make a selfish or self-centered decision.

Having a high level of both Empathy and Assertiveness is better than having an imbalance between the two, or having low levels of both. So in developing a balance, it is essential to avoid lowering your strength in one aspect to create a balance. If you feel you have an imbalance between these two competencies, acknowledge the impact of your imbalance and build up the weaker side for your own benefit, as well as for the greater good of the team.

Interpersonal Relationships-Independence Imbalance

Now, let's look at an imbalance between two other subscales: Interpersonal Relationships and Independence. You may recall from Chapter 4 that Interpersonal Relationships are our desire and ability to build and maintain mutually beneficial relationships, while Independence refers to our ability to act independently, make our own decisions, and stand up for what we believe in.

At first glance, these two subscales might appear to be mutually exclusive, but that is not the case.

When the Interpersonal Relationships scale is low and Independence is high, a leader may choose to make decisions without consulting their group. Because they are so independent and they don't see the need or role for Interpersonal Relationships, they don't feel the need to connect with their group or consider the needs of the group at all. They will often have less concern about how a decision might impact others.

In situations like this, the leader's self-direction and desire to act alone will override any need to leverage the Interpersonal Relationships they have. This can lead to isolated decision making and alienation of the group. Not only does the leader not garner support from their team, but the team itself feels disrespected. Leaders who behave like this often experience tunnel-like vision that results in their inability to take other people's perspectives and opinions into consideration.

However, when a leader has low Independence and high Interpersonal Relationship scores, leaders are less able to make decisions and rely too heavily on others for support when making decisions and taking action. This imbalance can put too much pressure on the team and cause the leader to waver in their decisions.

Another side effect is that the leader often puts too much emphasis on how the team views them. They worry about how well-liked they are, so their decisions often reflect what the team wants, rather than what it needs. Often, a leader's job is to make tough decisions, but in cases like this, the leader won't be able to make those decisions and may end up allowing people to walk all over them.

Alternatively, their emphasis on Interpersonal Relationships may lead to avoiding problems and letting too many issues slide out of fear of hurting their relationships with others. In my experience, many leaders struggle with balancing wanting to be liked with their need to make tough decisions.

When Interpersonal Relationships and Independence Are Balanced

When Interpersonal Relationships and Independence are balanced, a leader will be comfortable acting on their own, while adequately valuing and respecting the input and opinions of others. They will be able to build and maintain relationships with their team members and remain confident that their decisions and choices will not negatively affect those relationships.

Whilst they will value the Interpersonal Relationships they have with their team members, they also know that there is a job to be done and that sometimes they will have to take actions or make decisions that people on the team may not like. Rather than hiding from these situations and decisions, they confidently choose what is best for the team and its goals.

They rest assured that their relationships will continue to grow and improve, regardless of the decisions they have to make. The balance between Independence and Interpersonal Relationships can be one that is difficult to find. Often, leaders will choose one over the other to value more, but an imbalance between these two can lead to isolation, alienation, and ineffectiveness.

Just like with Assertiveness and Empathy, the ideal would be a high score in both, rather than one over the other, or two low scores. So if you do find or suspect an imbalance between these subscales, the key will be to build one up to meet the level of the other. Consider areas with the greatest imbalances the ones you need to focus on the most.

What Should Be Balanced?

Over the past few sections we have gone through some examples of EQ imbalances in action, but we have only looked at four subscales in particular: Assertiveness, Empathy, Interpersonal Relationships, and Independence. So what about the other 11?

Ideally, all EQ subscales would be in balance with each other. So, if you have a score of 70 in social responsibility, for example, you have between 60 and 80 in all other competencies. However, complete balance across the board is highly unlikely. In all my years studying and assessing EQ, I have not seen anyone demonstrate perfect balance.

Although we can speak about ideals, the reality is that purely balancing each of the 15 EQ competencies creates a highly complex and nearly impossible challenge. Ensuring your level with each competency is roughly the same across the board, would mean that if you have a high level in one, you would have to raise your level in all 14 other subscales.

Instead of this, the creators of the EQ-i model have established the key balance groupings for each subscale. By that, I mean that for every subscale, there are three other subscales we strive to balance. So, instead of trying to balance all 15 at the same time, you can work toward balancing one with its three counterparts.

Key Subscale Balances

The key subscale balances are the sets of subscales that are ideally balanced. A reference chart is available in the online resources section. For now, let's take a look at just one example: the Self-Expression composite.

As you know from Chapter 4, there are three subscales in the Self-Expression composite: Emotional Expression, Assertiveness, and Independence. Each of these subscales has three other subscales identified as their key balances.

Self-Expression Composite	Emotional Expression	Interpersonal Relationships
		Assertiveness
		Empathy
	Assertiveness	Interpersonal Relationships
		Emotional Self-Awareness
		Empathy
	Independence	Problem Solving
		Emotional Self-Awareness
		Interpersonal Relationships

So, for example, if we look at Emotional Expression, it is most importantly balanced with Interpersonal Relationships, Assertiveness, and Empathy. What this means is that ideally we would like to see roughly the same level of Emotional Expression in an individual as we would Interpersonal Relationships, Assertiveness or Empathy. Again it is important to consider that in a perfect world we would like Emotional Expression to be in balance with all of the other EQ subscales, however these key subscale balances help us understand some priorities when it comes to development.

When examining the Key Subscale Balances chart, you will notice that in some cases, these Key Subscale Balances are two-way – in other words the subscale is balanced with another subscale and that the balance works in reverse as well. However, this is not the case for all subscales and their key balances, so don't be concerned if you don't see the balance working both ways. There is a downloadable version of this chart on the Resources page for this book: http://myeqcoach.com/lgeibook

As you begin to plan your EQ development in Chapter 6, it is worth considering what you believe your areas of strength to be and where you would want to see improvement, and which Key Subscale Balances will help you make those improvements.

Emotional Well-Being

Emotional well-being refers to our general, overall emotional health at the present time. Well-being is considered to be a circular concept. In other words, higher levels of emotional intelligence contribute to emotional well-being and emotional well-being contributes to higher levels of emotional intelligence.

There is a distinction here, though, that emotional well-being is considered to vary over time. It might be that although someone's underlying emotional intelligence is high, they are currently experiencing some challenges in their life which affect their day-to-day emotional well-being. Therefore, emotional well-being is viewed as a state, in that it will fluctuate and change over time, as opposed to a trait, which would measure similarly at any given point in time.

Put more simply, everyone has bad days and bad months, but the bad days or months don't necessarily affect a person's underlying emotional intelligence.

They may just affect their emotional well-being, and therefore, how their EI is *displayed* on a day-to-day basis. We will discuss this in more detail in Chapter 8.

While emotional well-being is measured as a separate part of the emotional intelligence construct, it is recognized that some subscales have more potential for impacting emotional well-being than others. And as with everything in the EQ-i model, that impact can be positive or negative. The subscales that influence emotional well-being the most are Self-Regard, Interpersonal Relationships, Self-Actualization, and Optimism.

As you may recall from our discussions, Self-Regard refers to the way in which we look at ourselves, both the good and the bad. When you are experiencing low emotional well-being, it is easy for your Self-Regard to suffer. So in order to maintain positive Self-Regard, it is important to maintain positive emotional well-being.

Low Self-Regard can cause one to be harder on themselves and potentially lead to lower self-esteem, which can negatively impact your emotional well-being. So, developing your Self-Regard should be a priority when it comes to supporting your emotional well-being, particularly during difficult times.

Interpersonal Relationships play an important part in emotional well-being as well. As social animals, human beings rely on other people for interaction and support. In having an ability to build and maintain Interpersonal Relationships, you have a better chance at maintaining positive emotional well-being.

On the other side of that, then, is that negative emotional well-being can impact your ability to build and maintain Interpersonal Relationships. Being aware of this and taking action to mitigate these effects can help you avoid a negative cycle.

Self-Actualization, which refers to our ability to set and attain meaningful goals, plays an important role in emotional well-being as the process of planning and identifying solutions to challenges or issues is an important coping mechanism. So, when you suffer from lower emotional well-being, your Self-Actualization can suffer and you no longer push yourself to identify solutions. Further, having low Self-Actualization can contribute to negative feelings, as you can get lost in challenges and problems when you can't plan or identify solutions. Boosting your Self-Actualization can positively impact your emotional well-being.

Finally, and perhaps obviously, Optimism has a role to play as well, as it supports our ability to be positive about the future and understand that tough times will pass. On one side, emotional well-being is negatively affected when you can't see an upside or the light at the end of the tunnel. So, building up your Optimism will help you build up your emotional well-being. On the other side, as well, negative emotional well-being can greatly affect your ability to be optimistic.

Lower levels of emotional well-being can create a negative reinforcing cycle as it inhibits your competency in these four key areas, which are the areas that can best help you cope with challenges and tough times. Intervening in any or all of these four competencies can, in fact, help you reverse your negative reinforcing cycle. Building up these competencies before you find yourself struggling emotionally can help you mitigate or even avoid negative emotional well-being altogether.

If you have a concern for your own emotional well-being – perhaps you're going through a tough time, or you would like to improve your ability to cope – consider how learning more about, and improving, one or all of these four key areas may have a positive impact on your current well-being and improve your ability to maintain a healthy emotional state.

Summary

Overall, each EQ subscale is most effective if in balance with all the others. In this chapter, we examined how these balances and imbalances can impact your effectiveness as a leader.

As we look to developing emotional intelligence, understanding and exploring imbalances in our EQ is an important first step. But, as mentioned, we never work to reduce or diminish any area of EQ. Instead we look to balancing subscales to make sure we are not negatively over-demonstrating an area of emotional intelligence.

The key to building your emotional intelligence and improving your overall emotional quotient will be in attempting to find the right balance of each of your competencies. This will be crucial to establishing a plan for EQ development, which we will discuss further in the next chapter.

Additional resources and exercises are available online at http://myeqcoach.com/lgeibook

Section 2: Homework

EQ Subscale Reflection

Now that you have a better understanding of the subscales in the EQ-i model, think about and reflect on your current areas of strength and ones you need to develop. You'll do this by considering each subscale individually, then coming up with examples from your life that demonstrate strength in this area, and ones that show you need more development. If it's a development area, you can also identify whether it's a high- medium-, or low- priority area for you. This prioritization will be useful when we come to the development planning in Chapters 6 and 7.

You'll find a worksheet for EQ Subscale Reflection on the Resources webpage for this book. On the worksheet, you'll see a table for each of the 15 subscales in the EQ-i model, much like the table pictured below.

Self-Regard - is respecting oneself while understanding and accepting one's strengths and weaknesses. Self-regard is often associated with feelings of inner strength and self-confidence.				
What examples can you give where you demonstrated strength in this area?				
What examples can you give that demonstrate a need to develop in this area?				
Taking everything into consideration, do you feel that Self-Regard is one of your stronger areas of EQ, or an area where you need to develop? Is this a High, Medium, or Low priority for you? (Circle one)				
Development Area	High Priority	Medium Priority	Low Priority	**Strength Area**

What do I do with it?

1. In the top box, note down examples or stories about how you demonstrate strength in this area.

2. In the box below, note down examples of situations that demonstrate a need to develop in this area of EQ.

3. Once you have completed your reflections, use the section at the bottom of the table to indicate whether this is a strength area or a development area. If you believe you need more development, also indicate whether it's a high-, medium- or low- priority.

There is a table on the very last page of the worksheet that you can use to tabulate all of your responses across the 15 subscales.

Keep in mind that because there are 15 subscales in the EQ-i model, reflecting on all of them will take some time. To break things up, I would advise you to tackle no more than 2 or 3 subscales each day. In the morning, before you start your day, make a note of which subscales you will be reflecting on and thinking about that day. Then, at the end of the day, set some time aside to note down your reflections or thoughts on those susbcales. You'll find this approach much more practical than trying to work your way through the entire activity in one go.

As with all of the other reflective activities, honesty is the key. You will get most value from this exercise if you take a good hard look at yourself. That's not to say you need to be negative, or hard on yourself. Far from it. But, it is important to own up to the areas where you need to grow, as well as those where you are already strong.

As always if you have questions about homework please email us at info@myeqcoach.com.

Additional resources and exercises are available online at http://myeqcoach.com/lgeibook

Section 3

Developing Your Emotional Intelligence

6

The Basics of
EQ Development

In the past few chapters, we have examined emotional intelligence and its importance for effective leadership. We also learned about the EQ-i model and the value of balance between subscales. Equipped with that knowledge, it's now time to start exploring how you can develop your emotional intelligence and emotional effectiveness.

The question of whether or not one can actually develop their emotional intelligence is something I am asked about quite frequently, so we will start by exploring that topic and answering the question. Then, we will look at the best methods for developing EQ and the role of reflection, observation, and assessment in that process.

Let's start by first understanding if and why we can develop EI.

Can You Really Develop Your Emotional Intelligence?

We know from research into neuroplasticity that the brain is able to rewire itself if it is given persistent reinforcing stimuli. If you apply or enact a new behavior and do so repeatedly, the brain will rewire itself into this new way of being. The more often you do it and the longer you do it for, the more ingrained or permanent that behavior will become.

When I first started learning about neuroplasticity, I was told to think about it through an analogy of a path in the woods. Imagine you live in a cabin and every day you walk a mile down a well-worn path to the river to catch fish to eat. You've been walking down the same path for many years and so it's second nature – you don't even think about it.

Now, a friend who lives nearby tells you that a mile to the east of your cabin there is a lake, and that lake contains the most delicious fish – far tastier than the ones from the river. You're not sure that this could be true, but you're intrigued by the idea. The problem is the path to the lake is non-existent. In order to get there, you have to fight your way through the brambles and brush, but the promise of this delicious fish is enough that you decide to go for it.

The first time, the journey through the brush is very hard indeed and you consider giving up. When you get to the lake, though, the fish are plentiful and after battling your way back through the brush to your cabin, you cook the fish to find that they truly are delicious.

The next day, you are faced with the choice to use the well-worn path to the river or to once again fight your way through the brush to the lake. Because the fish tasted better from the lake – a more desirable result – you start back through the brush once more. Because of the work you did creating a path yesterday, the journey is slightly easier, but not by much.

The next day and the day after that, you consciously make that journey to the lake. Over time, the path becomes clear of brush and weeds. This has become your new path. And what has happened to the path to the river? It's become overgrown because you haven't used it. In some ways it isn't really identifiable as a path at all.

Just like with the cabin and paths, neuroplasticity allows us to create new habits. At first, they might be difficult, but the promise of a better life or better results helps us push through. After continual practice, we start to feel the new behaviors come more naturally and the old ones nearly disappear like an overgrown path. As much as it might be a simplification of neuroplasticity, it's a good analogy to keep in mind as you develop your EQ. You will have to make conscious choices about taking new paths, even when they are not natural or easy.

So, in essence, yes. You can definitely work to improve your emotional intelligence. While some people may be naturally more optimistic or empathetic, or have been raised more socially responsible or independent, each area of emotional intelligence can be developed and improved upon. It takes effort and a strong will to create new habits and new behaviors, but the payoff in the end is well worth it. As long as you know where you are, where you want to be, and why you want to be there, you can work to get there. These are the ideas we'll explore throughout the next few chapters.

There is something you'll need to be careful of. Plasticity does not differentiate between good and bad change. If you were to start demonstrating a negative behavior, such as habitual lying, your brain could just as easily implement this change as though it is something more positive. So, be careful about the changes you choose to implement.

The Gym Analogy

While neuroplasticity explains how the brain changes with new and repeated stimuli, the next important consideration is what the development process looks like to create the change we seek. To better understand that, I would like to offer you another analogy – this time we're going to the gym.

When you go to a gym for the first time, you will usually be put through some kind of assessment to determine where you are with your fitness. With the baseline understood, you can then work with a trainer to identify meaningful and attainable goals. Then, with the goals set, you can understand which activities will be needed for you to reach those goals and how much and how often you'll need to do them.

But effective exercise routines do not just focus on one part of your body. That's why you may have heard people talk about 'leg' days or 'arm' days – a good exercise regime may focus on one area of the body at a time, but not the same area at every workout. Having days assigned to different parts of your body ensures that you don't work the same set of muscles all the time. By changing it up, you will end up exercising all parts of your body in a week.

If you went to the gym and only worked on your arms every day, you'd get a couple of interesting results. First of all, your arms would definitely get bigger. But because you were not working your legs or your core, you would likely find that the usefulness of all the extra strength in your arms would be limited, as other areas of your body would not have been complementarily developed. Perhaps more worryingly, you would likely find that while your arms could sustain a certain activity or weight, the rest of your body could not, which could result in injury. Overall fitness is increased over time by working the different parts of your body in proportion and relation with each other. This creates the best and most balanced results.

When you go to the gym, one of the most important rules to follow is that you don't try to do too much, too quickly. If you are lifting weights, for example, you would start with more repetitions and lighter weights before moving on to heavier weights and fewer repetitions.

Developing physical fitness requires perseverance. In the early days, you are likely to feel sore and fatigued. You may feel discouraged because its hard and not that enjoyable. You may also notice that your attendance at the gym impacts your social life, because you have to take time away from friends and family. These things can conspire together and result in you giving up. However, if you want to get results, you need to keep at it. Over time, you become stronger, get less sore, and find that your social agenda begins to accommodate or even complement your gym attendance. I won't go as far as saying you will enjoy going to the gym, but for many people this does happen.

As you reach your first few fitness goals, you celebrate your success and mark that you've been progressing in the right direction. If your goals are realistic, this should serve to reinforce the practicality and viability of your fitness plan, which in turn will help motivate you to keep it as part of your daily practice. It will support you in setting your next goal, which may be to simply maintain your new-found level of fitness.

When we think about developing emotional intelligence, all of the same principles apply. You need to start your EQ development by understanding where you are. Then, set clear, practical, and meaningful goals. You need to ensure you don't overwork one area of your emotional intelligence or try and do too much too fast. You need to persevere and keep at it, even when it is tough or taxing. When you achieve your goals, you need to celebrate that success to keep yourself on track and motivated for future changes.

If you make your EQ development part of your daily leadership practice, you are more likely to achieve your goals. There is no such thing as having finished your EQ development. Just like with the gym, if you stop practicing, you are likely to fall back into your old habits. You will lose the benefits you gained and your brain will rewire itself back to those old paths.

So when you look at your development plan, think about it like physical fitness or development. Although you might not see the results the same way, you will notice improvement in your leadership and emotional development.

Just like at the gym, the process of developing your emotional intelligence must start with understanding where you are. That's where the ROAD to Success comes in.

The ROAD to Success - Reflection, Observation, Assessment, Development

Much like how going to the gym will improve your fitness, developing a process of reflection, observation and assessment will help you develop your EQ and improve your overall leadership and emotional well-being. By making the plan concrete – by writing it down – you will be able to track your progress over time. But, before you get to the development, you need to first figure out what to work on. For that, we follow what I call the ROAD to Success: Reflection, Observation, Assessment, and Development.

To structure this process, we use the following model.

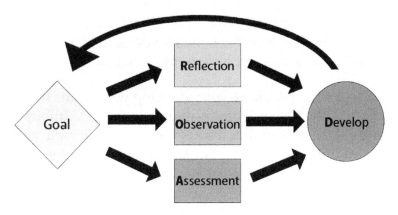

Your ROAD to Success will start by first identifying a goal. You'll use the processes of reflection, observation, and assessment to establish a baseline. Then, once you know where you are and where you want to be, you can begin to develop in pursuit of your goals. Being clear on this initial goal will help you plot your course and serve as motivation throughout the development process.

Let's take a look at each of these elements in more detail.

Identifying Your Goals

Stephen Covey, the late, great leadership and productivity author, said in his book, *The 7 Habits of Highly Effective People*, to always begin with the end in mind. There really is no better advice than that when it comes to developing emotional intelligence.

Clarity of your goals, both the big ones and smaller ones is, quite simply, a critical part of the development process. Yet, you'd be surprised at how often people don't put sufficient thought into their goal. People often set goals that are too broad to be useful or ones that are unrealistic. Goals like, 'I want to develop my emotional intelligence,' 'I want to become a better leader,' or 'I want to be CEO within 5 years' might be nice to imagine, but they don't set you up for success.

Being clear and realistic about your goals will increase your chances of achieving them. It sounds slightly circular, but without goals you won't know what you're working toward and you won't know when you are getting close to achieving them or when your process is getting off track. As I mentioned in the gym analogy, celebrating your success is an important part of development and so you'll need to be clear in your goals to know when you've reached them so you can celebrate.

The clearer you are with where you want to be, the easier it will be to determine the path you want to take. When you know where you are and where you want to be, it will be much easier to develop strategies to get you there.

Here's an example. Let's say you want to become more assertive in your team so that your ideas are heard instead of ignored. You could set a goal like, 'I want to be more assertive,' but that won't get you very far. Instead, you take some time to reflect and observe your own behavior, and you find that you speak up about your opinions approximately one time for every five meetings you attend. You consider it and determine that you want to speak up more often, so you set a goal, like 'I will speak up at least once at each meeting.' Now, you have a clear and quantifiable goal. You will know when it happens because you can count how many times, but it is still realistic as you are not drastically changing your behavior all at once. Perhaps future goals will help you work on further increasing the frequency or quality of your comments, but for now you keep it simple and straightforward.

A great way to ensure that your goals are clear and realistic is to use the SMART goal setting principle. SMART means your goals are Specific, Measurable, Attainable, Relevant, and Time-Bound. You will find a worksheet in the online resources that can help you with setting SMART goals.

Sources of Inspiration

Another question I am often asked is "What should I work on?" The answer though, cannot come from me, or anyone else for that matter. Identifying which areas of your leadership and emotional intelligence you want to work on should not be determined by another person. It has to be something that is important and meaningful to you.

The previous exercises in this book can help you identify what some of your development goals could be. Look back at *Your Leadership Landscape*, and *Future You* from Section 1 and the *EQ Subscale Reflection* from Section 2. These exercises can provide some inspiration for areas of your leadership you would like to develop.

However, I want to caution you. If you simply pick an area of emotional intelligence that you want to develop from the *EQ Subscale Reflection*, but you have not identified a broader goal that you would like to work on first, you will struggle with your development. The simple reason for this is that as human beings we tend to be motivated more by working toward a goal that will improve our situation, or create some other outcome we are looking for rather than simply developing something for the sake of it. But, what goals to work on? Ultimately, your goals should stem from a simple question: what would you like to do differently?

Reflection

Once you have defined your goals, it's time to start down the ROAD to Success. The first stop on that road is Reflection.

Reflection focuses on taking time out from your leadership to think about, or reflect on, what is working and what is not in your daily life with specific reference to your goal. Essentially, you should be thinking about and understanding what would best contribute to that goal and the factors that influence your beliefs, behaviors, and actions around that goal.

Although many people consider reflection a major event that happens only periodically, the best and most effective reflection practices happen on a regular basis. Setting aside some time daily to reflect will help you keep track of where you are and where you are heading.

Some good questions to ask yourself are:

- What was the best thing about today / the last week?
- What went well, why, and what was my part in

121

it?

- What did not go so well, why, and what was my part in it?
- Which relationships went as well, or better than I expected. Why, and what was my part in it?
- Which relationships did not go as well as I had hoped. Why, and what was my part in it?
- What key learning can I take away from today / this last week that will help me to be as, or more successful tomorrow / next week?

Rather than simply sitting around and thinking, reflection is about being honest with yourself about your behavior and your progress with your goal. Take this as a time to ask yourself these tough questions and think through how you will continue to make progress. Consider patterns in your behavior and your leadership that may contribute to or work against your goal.

Reflective Journaling

Sometimes, when I talk to groups of leaders from traditionally hard professions, like engineering or sales, the idea of keeping a journal is viewed like keeping a personal diary. It sounds like a soft practice, which seems pointless to them. They can often see value for other people, but don't see where it is relevant to themselves. Nothing could be further from the truth.

Keeping a journal, especially when done on a daily basis, is an effective way to reflect on and understand what is going on in your leadership, and your life more broadly. It helps us to not only recall more accurately what happened each day, but to think events through and analyze them on a higher level than is possible when you are actually experiencing them. Journaling is actually quite cathartic, with people often reporting that they've had incredible realizations about situations, events, or patterns of their own behavior while journaling on a regular basis.

Research suggests that handwriting your journal not only slows down your thinking, but it also helps you remember or cement knowledge more effectively than typing. Slowing down your thinking lets your brain more fully process your thoughts and make connections between events and ideas that it may simply not have time to make at regular thinking speed. If you are going to journal, I suggest you use a paper-based book rather than typing notes on a computer. Although it can be cost effective and save space, some people find typing notes on a computer or tablet to be too much like work and it doesn't allow you to slow down and consider each event as you write. I know the last thing I want to do at the end of a long day is sit at a keyboard.

When it comes to journaling, there really is no one right way of doing it. If it helps to have an electronic reminder to start your reflection or it is simply easier to carry around an app on your phone than a physical journal, make whatever choice is best for you. The most important thing is that whatever method you choose helps you form a habit and allows you to make journaling a regular practice.

If the idea of keeping a daily journal seems onerous, consider less frequent journaling or other types of reflective practices. Many leaders choose to start out journaling only once a week and take that time to reflect on the previous seven days. While you might find your memory fades or you have a more difficult time capturing your emotions, a weekly practice might help you see how a daily journal can be easy to do and effective. Alternatively, you could consider only writing down your thoughts or feeling when something significant happens.

If you are interested in this kind of reflection, I have included a Reflection worksheet to the online resources for this section. Any journaling is better than doing no reflection at all.

Along these lines, not everyone feels comfortable writing down their thoughts and ideas. Other reflective practices like meditation and discussion can incorporate reflection into your day without journaling. Additional suggestions and tools can be found in the online resources section.

Observation

The next stop on our ROAD to Success process is Observation. Observation, as you may imagine, is the process of watching what is happening in order to understand and learn from it. We can think about observation in two ways: observation of self, and observation of others. Let's look at them separately.

Observation of Self

Observation of self is not an easy practice, but it's an absolutely critical part of your EQ development. Only you know what's going on in your own head, and only you can make sense of what is driving your actions and behaviors. Why DID you help that person, but not someone else? Why DIDN'T you speak up at the meeting? Why DID you make that comment? Self-observation is the skill of becoming aware of your thoughts, actions, reactions, and behaviors in the moment so you can better understand which processes are triggered and why.

Early on, when I first started working my own EQ development, I quickly realized which situations were strong triggers for me emotionally and that, when triggered, I would behave defensively. By developing my self-observation skills over time, I was able to develop a sense of when I was being triggered and began using my internal dialogue as an alert. In more practical terms, as I sensed myself beginning to be triggered by a situation, I would simply say to myself, "It's happening again. Slow down. Be careful." These few words were enough to help me take control of the situation and ensure that I could react in the most appropriate way.

Self-observation requires that you do what you are doing while also watching yourself doing these things, and it can take quite a lot of practice to do well. The best way to connect with your inner observer it's to recognize the voice inside your head. And, as the old joke goes, if you are thinking "I don't know what he means by the voice inside your head," THAT'S the voice I am talking about. By recognizing this voice, and the role it plays in your day-to-day existence, you listen to what it is saying and use it as an observer.

If you want to learn more about the voice, and how it does and does not help you, I recommend you pick up a copy of *Taming Your Gremlin* by Rick Carson. This book may be over 30 years old (though it has been updated a number of times), but it is still the best resource I have ever seen for better understanding and dealing with the voice inside your head.

Observation of Others

Observation of others is also an effective way to help guide your emotional intelligence development. By noticing what other people do in situations, you can learn what you perceive to be good and bad demonstrations emotional intelligence. You can also begin to see strategies and consider ideas that might work for you and your own development. You can even identify 'champions' – people who you believe to be very strong in certain areas of EI – and use these people as role models and examples to help with your development. Understand, though, that I don't mean you should mimic what others do, but rather take them as an example of what you might consider doing and seeing what may and may not work for you.

When you observe others (and by the way, make sure it isn't creepy!) watch how they deal with situations and interact with others. What words do they use? How congruent is their body language with their words? To what extent do they adapt their communication or conversation style in relation to others? What do you think is going on for them in their mind? What kind of outcomes are they driving towards, and do they reach them?

Observation augmented by reflection through journaling is the best way to identify patterns and potential avenues for development. By observing and reflecting, you can follow your own behavior, find models for changing that behavior, recognize the progress you are making, and find inspiration for new goals. Along with these tools, Assessment can provide a concrete way to draw connections and develop a plan for success.

Assessment

The next step on the ROAD to Success is Assessment. In this context, we are referring to an Assessment of where you are at with the various elements of emotional intelligence that relate to your goals. The Assessment phase is when you start to put it all together and determine where you are with your EQ subscales and which ones you want to focus on. Now, you can begin to 'map' those subscales to the goals you are working on.

Here is an example. Imagine your goal is to contribute more to the ideas and work of your team. Which EQ subscales might be associated with that? In Chapter 4, you will recall we covered the definitions and functions of each of the subscales.

If you want your ideas heard on the team, it's likely that you would want to develop your Assertiveness, as it helps with putting forth your ideas and opinions.

You would also want to look at Independence, as it helps you see the value of your ideas and mitigates the impact that criticism might have. Third, you might want to develop Empathy, as it helps your ability to see other people's perspectives and stances on an issue. With all three of these, you will be able to more effectively propose ideas, be confident in those ideas, and present those ideas in a way that is better suited for your team's needs. There would, of course, be other subscales that you might identify as well, but these will do as a starting point.

With the subscales identified, you can ask yourself questions like, where am I on that subscale? What would it look like if I was higher? What does my current story look like? What would my success story look like? What do others think of my skills in this subscale, and who might I be able to ask for feedback? You should also refer back to the *EQ Subscale Reflection* you completed in Section 2.

Taking these questions into consideration will allow you to more accurately determine where you are on the subscales you are hoping to work on. If you want to delve further into where you might be, consider participating in an EQ360 or EQ-i assessment. These psychometric assessments are validated by the developers of the EQ-i model, and can help you get a solid understanding of where your strengths lie and which areas you might seek to develop. For more information about these assessments, see *Taking Your EQ Development to The Next Level* in Closing Thoughts at the end of the book.

Action – We're Getting to That

With the Reflection, Observation, Assessment stages now complete, your next stop on the ROAD to success is, of course, Development. In the next chapter, I will introduce you to an effective process for finalizing your plan and putting it into action.

While it may be tempting to move to actions before completing the reflection, observation, and assessment stages, you should exercise some caution. When you move to action too quickly, you may find that the actions you have identified are inappropriate, or that you're working on subscales you already excel in. You may also find that you are more easily distracted and set off course. If you truly want to succeed at developing your EQ, you need to do the foundational work before you take the bigger steps.

Summary

Most leaders take don't take the time they need to make a realistic assessment of their leadership. If you are going to take your development seriously, you'll need to do some preparation work by reflecting, observing, and assessing your leadership before you launch into development.

Reflection is a process of looking at your world and figuring out what's going well, and what could be going differently. Observation of yourself, and others, helps you to identify the thoughts, actions, and behaviors you are displaying relative to your leadership. However, do keep in mind that your view of these thoughts, actions, and behaviors is through the lens of your own perception. As we discussed earlier in this book, these perceptions may be colored by your mental models, or core values and beliefs.

Finally, Assessment of which EQ subscales you need to work on, and a realistic evaluation of where you are on those subscales is critical to making sure your development plan is working on the right things. With those steps completed, you can now move to developing your Actions, which we will talk about in the next chapter.

Additional resources and exercises are available online at http://myeqcoach.com/lgeibook

7

Putting Your Plan into Action

At this point, you should have a solid idea of which EQ subscales you want to work on to meet your goals. The next step is to identify the actions you will need to take to help you on your path to Development. We do this using the EQ 1-2-3 development process, which helps guide your choices and actions using Microresolutions. Let's take a deeper look into EQ 1-2-3 and the factors that will contribute to your success.

The EQ 1-2-3 Development Process

When I first started working with leaders and their emotional intelligence, I discovered that while they knew they wanted to make changes, they were not sure how to structure their development in a meaningful way. The leaders I worked with at the beginning were not sure what to work on, and when they did find one thing to develop, they often didn't know where to go after that. To provide a simple, sustainable plan, I created the EQ 1-2-3 development process.

The EQ 1-2-3 process is designed to help you create a practice for your EQ development. I have called this the EQ 1-2-3 process because it works like this:

1. Choose 1 area or subscale of your emotional intelligence to develop.
2. For a period of 2 weeks…
3. Commit to 3 small actions that you will work to implement.

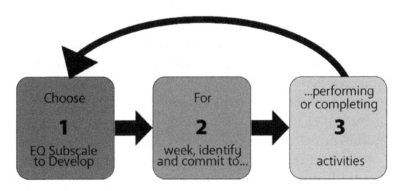

By making you focus on one area at a time, and then committing to a specific time period, you are much more likely to complete the three tasks you have identified.

Before we look at the EQ 1-2-3 process in more detail, there are a few points I want to make. First, the EQ development process is not a quick fix. Just like creating a new path in the woods, it takes time and commitment if you are to succeed. Keeping with it will help you build new habits and neural pathways that will eventually make these changes easier to implement.

Second, no one succeeds at everything they try, especially with EQ development. But don't let that discourage you. The key will be to find your way around roadblocks and persevere through challenges. It will be worth it in the long run. And finally, while the EQ 1-2-3 process can be applied to immediate goals and outcomes, it works best as a long-term development process. For best results, keep the process going indefinitely.

EQ 1: Pick One Area to Develop

The EQ 1-2-3 process starts by first picking one EQ-i subscale that you want to develop. You'll recall from our discussion in Chapter 6 that part of the assessment process is to determine which subscales you need to work on to meet your goals. You can determine these either through Reflection and Observation, or by taking an EQ-i or EQ360 assessment. Even though your goal may require that you develop multiple areas of your emotional intelligence, for now, just choose one subscale to develop at a time.

The reason for this is simple: you are much more likely to stay committed to, remember, and reflect on the success or failure of a small number of activities, rather than a larger number of activities across different areas of emotional intelligence. By focusing in on one area of emotional intelligence, you can ensure the work you have to do remains manageable and consistent.

When you choose too many areas of EQ to work on at a time, there is a much higher chance that you will give up and forget the process entirely. That's the nature of over commitment. To borrow from our gym analogy in Chapter 6, you will most certainly get better fitness results if you go to yoga and spin classes and do a full workout at the gym every day, but can you really sustain that pace and commitment? Not likely. It's the same with your EQ development. Slow and steady wins the race every time.

EQ 2-3: For Two Weeks, Do Three Things

Now that you have chosen a subscale, the next step is to find three activities that will help you develop that area of your emotional intelligence. We call these small actions Microresolutions. They are real, tangible and specific activities geared toward helping you develop and improve on one subscale. For example, if you were working on your Impulse Control, it might be that you will write down your critique of someone else's idea at a meeting, rather than voicing it immediately. These small acts are the core of developing your EQ.

When you are developing your actions, you will want to make them small, practical, and doable. We call this kind of action a 'Microresolution' because they are small actions designed to hone in on a very specific behavioral change. The more specific the better. The book, *Small Move, Big Change* by Caroline Arnold is a great way to learn more in general about Microresolutions and how they can be used to create the kind of change you want to see in your leadership and your life. The book demonstrates how small, simple things, like taking a moment to organize paperwork, can create dramatic shifts in your life. Using small, doable actions lets you create simple sustainable practices that can help you achieve much larger, and longer term goals.

As you can see, these actions are not complex. In fact, that's the point. They are simple, doable actions that anyone can implement. Although greater, more overt actions might seem to result in long-term change, don't underestimate the power of simple. When you plan simple actions, you are more likely to actually do them and take that chance. With bigger actions, you will find yourself too intimidated or nervous to practice that action on a regular basis.

So, if we are trying to keep it simple, why, you might ask, are there three activities? Well, the reason for that is that in some cases, or on some days, you may not get to perform one of your activities. And some are only intended to be performed once or twice in the two-week period, like reaching out to a new contact. By having a small number of different activities to work on, you can vary your activities over the two weeks while still keeping within your tight plan. When you don't have a chance to do one of the activities, you will still be able to do the others.

You will find a worksheet to help you develop your own EQ 1-2-3 plan in the online resources section for this book.

After the two-week period, you will move to another EQ-i subscale and for two weeks you will identify three actions that you will take for that subscale, and so on. This process can continue indefinitely as you work toward your goal. Now, instead of just switching from one to the next, you will compound these activities. So, even after you've moved on to week five or seven you will continue to practice your Microresolutions from week one. Over time, these new behaviors will become your default.

If you finish the two-week process and you're not sure of how to proceed, go back to your ROAD to Success to determine where to go next. If you feel you've achieved your goal, start the process over again to keep building on your development. The important thing to remember is that developing your EQ is an ongoing, iterative process.

To Get You Started

The secret to creating an effective development plan that works for you is learning to create and develop your own activities. The process for doing that is relatively simple, and I will walk you through some ideas for inspiration. However, I do want to get you started on your development plan right away, so you will find, in the online resources for this book (http://myeqcoach. com/lgeibook), a list of three suggested activities for each of the 15 subscales. There are sufficient activities here for one complete go-round of the EQ-i model. If you are following the EQ 1-2-3 process for each subscale, that's a 30-week development program!

Other Sources for Actions

You may find the sample actions I provided with this book don't appeal to you, or that you need more actions for your future development. The key to continual development of your emotional intelligence is to learn to develop these activities on your own.

There are many easy ways to find resources that might inspire your activities. Steven Stein and Howard Book's *The EQ Edge: Emotional Intelligence and Your Success* is a great read and follows the EQ-i 2.0 model. The book has a chapter that corresponds with each of the EQ subscales and outlines some suggested activities. Another option is to go through an EQ-i or EQ360 assessment process. These tools will not only give you a score for each of the 15 subscales, but they also provide suggestions for activities for improvement.

Perhaps the best way to choose actions is to simply use your common sense. If you take a few moments to come up with some activities for, for example increasing your Independence or Self-Actualization, it's quite easy to do. Some questions you can ask yourself to help develop your own actions might include:

- What would it look like if I did more of this?
- How might I do this differently?
- What great examples of this aspect of emotional intelligence have I seen others demonstrate (think back to the Observation phase)?
- Is there something I should stop doing in order to do this more (for example, indulging in negative self-talk)?

Here is a more direct example of how you can go about developing actions:

You learned earlier in this book that Independence is about your ability to live and act without being overly independent on others. So, making decisions on your own, undertaking activities by yourself, or developing interests separately from the people you know are great ways to develop your Independence. Simply generate a list of more specific activities based on these elements. The same goes for Self-Actualization. You already know that Self-Actualization relates to the setting and achievement of meaningful goals, so you can go about identifying Microresolutions by thinking of ways you might help yourself set and achieve small goals and develop a plan.

Once you have taken some time to familiarize yourself with each subscale, this process will become much easier. Again, reading books and articles on EQ can help in this regard. EQ development is a personal process, I can't tell you everything that will work because what works for you might not work as well for someone else. Learning to develop your own activities and take ownership of your personal development is essential for long-term success.

Developing Your Action Plan

When it comes to developing your plan, the best advice I can give is to start small and stay small to get big results. One of the mistakes I see leaders make when they embark on a process for EQ development is that they commit to actions that are so big they can't possibly do them. Another mistake is that after setting a small, suitable action, they find that they experience success with it and so they make the next action big, thinking that this new, bigger action will get even bigger results. But again, they generally fall foul of an action that's so big it's neither doable nor sustainable. So, keep that in mind – *Start Small, Stay Small, Get Big Results*.

In the online resources section, you will find an EQ 1-2-3 Action Plan template that has all of the 15 subscales listed, along with 3 slots to write in the actions you are going to commit to. Depending on your development goals, it might be that you don't make it through all of the subscales, or it might be that you complete an entire Action Plan over the course of 30 weeks and then start over again. Whatever your process, make sure that you are always working on the right thing (those subscales that are connected to your goals). Here is a quick summary of what you need to do to develop your EQ.

1. Identify which EQ subscale you are going to work on.

2. Identify or develop three activities you will complete.

3. Do those three activities as often as is practical/reasonable within that 2-week period.

Finally, don't worry if you don't get to all three things on your list. Some of them may well be situational. If, for example, you are working on your Assertiveness and one of your actions is to stand up for yourself in a difficult situation, it goes without saying that you shouldn't create a difficult situation just so you can complete the action. If one doesn't come up, focus on your other two actions.

As mentioned, you will find a blank template for your action plan in the online resources section. You can use this template to structure your activities. Again, as you develop your actions, remember that small, doable actions work best – often the smaller the better.

Motivation and The Change Equation

Identifying actions will be meaningless if you are not motivated to change. For many leaders, uncovering the motivation to change makes the difference between following your action plan and letting it sit on the shelf gathering dust.

While many leaders like the idea of developing emotional intelligence and see the potential value in doing so, many, if not all, find it challenging to actually do the work and implement change in pursuit of their EQ goals. But why?

Having worked with leaders for more than a decade on developing their leadership, I have come to realize that many are simply not dissatisfied enough with their current situation. They are not motivated enough to put in the work to develop and create change in their leadership. This lack of dissatisfaction effectively translates into a resistance to change.

Some time ago, I was introduced to the idea of the Change Equation. This concept was developed by David Gleicher in the 60's, and later refined by Kathie

Dannemiller in the 80's. The Change Equation suggests that, together, dissatisfaction with the present situation, a vision for the desired future state, and the first steps of the change process need to add up to and result in something stronger than the resistance for change.

While the Change Equation was targeted at organizational change initiatives, it works just as well for individuals who are looking to develop their EQ. To develop an effective change process, you must have a vision of what you want the change to be and understand the steps required to start working towards that change, but if the dissatisfaction is not there – if you are content with things as they are – you won't be sufficiently motivated to develop.

Put more simply, if you feel like you are already a great leader with little or no need for development, what is your motivation to improve? It is for this reason that my first questions with new clients, are: what is working? and what could work better?

As we discussed in Chapter 6, identifying your goal is a critical part of the development process, but simply inventing goals does not sufficiently motivate. We need to figure out the dissatisfaction element. How do you need your leadership to change in order for you to be effective? And what is your current level of effectiveness (or ineffectiveness) costing you in terms of deliverables?

Dissatisfaction: Uncovering Your Thirst

Some years ago, when discussing the effectiveness of a leadership development program I was designing, a mentor of mine said, "You can lead a horse to water but you can't make it drink." In that moment, I remember thinking, 'yes, I have heard that before.' But then she added, "if the horse is thirsty you won't need to." And that's the secret.

Telling you about a process to develop your emotional intelligence will not be sufficient motivation for you to go ahead and do it. You have to spend some time figuring out what it is you want to do – how you want to improve as a leader – before you begin the development process for yourself. Keep this in mind as you consider which actions you want to take.

Success...

The EQ 1-2-3 process is about creating a daily practice for your EQ development. As with anything else, whether its learning to play a musical instrument, working out, changing your diet, or improving your emotional effectiveness, success is the sum of small efforts repeated day in and day out. Its surprisingly easy, and surprisingly effective, if you can commit to it.

So, keep in mind – developing your EQ is an ongoing practice that takes time. You have to commit to doing something every day. Always keep in mind that small changes over a prolonged period of time will yield the best results, and finally, don't forget that you must Reflect, Observe, and Assess before you act.

Summary

Here is a quick rundown of the entire development process I have laid out in this, and the last chapter:

1. Determine which subscale you will work on by identifying a larger goal, and then reflecting on and observing your current thinking and behavior around that goal.

2. Determine which EQ subscales are related to that goal, and then Assess where you are at on that subscale.

3. Consider ways you would like to improve on this subscale.

4. Brainstorm and research actions that could contribute to building this subscale.

5. Do at least one of these actions every day for 2 weeks.

6. Pick another subscale that you identified in relation to the goal you are working towards and re-assess, or identify a new goal and choose the next subscale you will work on.

Additional resources and exercises are available online at http://myeqcoach.com/lgeibook

8

Maintaining Peak Emotional Effectiveness

So, your development plan is underway, but being the most emotionally effective leader you can takes more than just developing your EQ skills. You also need to take care of yourself as well. Day-to-day life events affect your emotional intelligence and your emotional well-being. No matter how emotionally intelligent you are, there are just some things that are unpredictable and difficult to handle. The best way to meet these challenges head-on is to set yourself up for success by taking care of yourself emotionally and physically. Let's start by looking at how just living your everyday life can impact your demonstrated EQ.

Any Given Monday

The phrase 'On any given Sunday' refers to how, in professional football, no matter what the anticipated outcome of the game, there are many factors that can influence the outcome. Borrowing from this phrase,

145

I often explain that when it comes to emotional intelligence, on any given Monday, it's hard to predict how things will go as there are many factors, both known and unknown, anticipated and unexpected, that will make a difference in how you progress and how you react.

Imagine two scenarios.

In the first scenario, it's Monday morning in late spring. You wake gently after 8 ½ hours of restful sleep, minutes before the alarm is due to go off. You start your day with some quiet meditation before preparing breakfast for you and your family. The kids are well-prepared for the day at school, especially as you made their lunch the night before and took time to ensure they had all the books they need for today's lessons. The kids playfully eat their breakfast and make it out to the curb a few minutes before the bus arrives to take them to school.

Your drive to work is pleasant with light traffic. The music on the radio gets you energized about the day ahead. When you arrive at the office, you are greeted with enthusiasm by your co-workers and when you check your calendar you see that you have only three one-hour meetings today with lots of time in between to catch up on emails and tackle that strategic plan you've been working on.

After grabbing a cup of herbal tea, you go to the first meeting. In 20 minutes, you've worked collaboratively with your peers to tackle all of the items on the agenda. After a few minutes of positive chitchat about the direction of the work, you head back to your office and settle in to work on your strategic plan.

Now if that scenario sounds like your world, then lucky you. For many people, a more realistic Monday morning might look like this:

Its Monday morning in mid-January. You awake to the screech of the alarm clock, your head feeling slightly fuzzy from the large glass of wine you drank last night just before bed.

Although you fell asleep quickly, in the middle of the night you spent an hour awake, staring at the ceiling while you mulled over how to best get the strategic plan done. Still, you feel somewhat rested. You make your way downstairs to find that the kids have already started to make their own breakfast. The kitchen looks like something from a reality TV cooking show, and not in a good way.

Realizing that you have forgotten to make the kids' lunches, you frantically piece together a somewhat nutritional lunchbox and usher the kids out to the curb just as the bus pulls up. You run back in the house to get yourself ready, before spending 10 minutes in the freezing cold to scrape ice off the car windows. As you start down the road towards work, you realize you're low on gas and will need to make a stop before you get too far. As the minutes tick by, you realize that while you won't be late for work, you also won't get a chance to spend any time wading through emails before your first meeting.

147

After gassing up, you join the long line of slow-moving traffic along the freeway. The chirpy music on the radio does little to help your mood, which is darkening quickly. After a frustrating journey, you arrive at your office to find that you are already five minutes late for your first meeting. Worse than that, a quick look at your agenda for the day shows that you are in back-to-back meetings for almost the entire day. It only takes a moment to realize that this means you will have no time to work on the strategic plan, especially as you will have to tend to your email backlog.

As you enter the meeting room, you prepare to apologize for your tardiness only to find your peers in a pitched battle over the direction of the new strategy. The rest of the hour is spent making little or no progress, resulting in a group of frustrated people. As you leave this meeting and head to the next, you come to the realization that you will be working late today just to make sure you are not too far behind tomorrow.

--

So, of course, neither of these is the case every day. The point is that you never really do know what to expect. Some days will be smoother and more productive than others. Even before you wake up each day, your emotional intelligence impacts how your day goes and how well you can roll with the punches. This is the same for everyone, whether they choose to accept it or not.

What's more is that how your day goes can impact how effective your emotional intelligence is. Just like with your emotional well-being, your day-to-day life can determine how independent, assertive, or empathetic you are. For example, a lack of sleep affects your ability to make decisions, while the stress induced by constantly being late creates challenges for your emotional sensitivity and emotional reactions. These things, when combined with other factors, affect and impact your emotional intelligence. Understanding this effect is an important part of becoming a more emotionally effectively leader.

Maximal vs. Demonstrated EQ

Although we just discussed how your day-to-day life can impact your emotional effectiveness, it's important to consider that it does not actually reduce your emotional intelligence. Instead, the impact is on your *demonstrated* EQ.

Think of it this way: everyone has a *maximal* level of EQ – in other words the highest levels of emotional intelligence they are capable of. So we could say each person has their own maximal level on each of the 15 subscales.

However, just because that's the maximum they are capable of, doesn't mean that they will actually operate at that level. Many things impact our demonstrated emotional intelligence, but some of the biggest and most common contributors are stress, caffeine, a lack of sleep or fatigue, and alcohol. We will take a look at each of these in more detail later in this chapter. For now, just remember that these factors can have an impact.

EQ Is Discretionary

Further complicating the maximal vs demonstrated EQ balance is that demonstrations of emotional intelligence are discretionary. One can *choose* to operate at the highest possible level of their EQ or not. To put it more simply, just because you *can* act a certain way doesn't mean you will. Again, circumstances and situations play a part here. For example, imagine that yesterday you had a very difficult interaction with one of your co-workers, and that you would like and expect that co-worker to apologize to you, but thus far the apology has not been forthcoming.

Today when you interact with that co-worker, even though you know how you should behave from a maximal EQ perspective, you may opt not to do that. In other words, you are discretionarily reducing your *demonstrated* emotional intelligence in your interactions with that co-worker because of your previous interactions with them.

Sometimes this discretionary reduction is subconscious and at other times it is quite conscious. Conscious adjustments in demonstrated EQ can be both positive and negative. In the positive, your discretion can be to produce situationally appropriate behavior, while in the negative, it can be used for manipulation and deception. As part of becoming a more emotionally effective leader you'll need to become aware of the difference between these two.

Now, let's take a look at some of the factors that can affect your demonstrated EQ on a day-to-day basis.

The Impact of Stress on EQ

It should come as no surprise that stress can have an impact on your emotional intelligence. This is such an important factor that Stress Management is a composite in the EQ-i model. The concept of stress comes from an engineering analogy. When something is placed under sufficient pressure by external factors, that thing deforms or changes shape. Think of a wooden shelf. When a heavy object is placed in the middle between two supports, the shelf will actually bow or change shape under that pressure.

The same thing happens to you and your emotional intelligence under stress. As the pressure mounts, your EQ will become deformed and change shape. In some cases, this deformation will cause you to increase your demonstrated EQ in some areas, and in other cases it will cause you to reduce it.

For example, it is not uncommon for someone who is emotionally in control under normal circumstances, to shout angrily at someone in a stressful situation. This exhibition of emotion would suggest an increased level of Emotional Expression, an increased level of Assertiveness, but a decreased level of Impulse Control and Empathy. If you were to look at this person's normal EQ profile and compare it to their profile under stress, you would see they can be quite different.

Managing stress is a challenge for many leaders, but it's an area where the simplest and time-tested solutions work best. These strategies include removing yourself from the source of stress, taking time to reflect on the situation and manage your emotional reactions, physical activity like walking or working out, meditative practices like yoga or structured breathing, or even just shifting your attention to something else.

If you are committed to becoming a more emotionally effective leader, you'll need to understand both the stress triggers that you're susceptible to as well as the stress management techniques that work best for you.

The Impact of Caffeine on EQ

Talking about caffeine can be a contentious topic. People who like caffeine tend to like it a lot, and while the research is mixed on whether caffeine is or is not good for your body, there is little debate about how the drug affects your emotions. Given the impact of caffeine on the brain, it's slightly ironic and even mildly amusing to think that in most work environments it is the most common drink.

While the mechanisms by which caffeine affects the brain, and subsequently our emotional intelligence, are complex, the results of those effects is relatively simple. Essentially, caffeine causes your brain to become more aroused and puts it into a fight or flight state which has both up- and downsides. The upsides are that in this aroused state, the brain can be more productive and has the potential to process information quicker. It also staves off the effects of fatigue. The downside, however, is that you become more emotionally sensitive, particularly to negative stimuli. You may also react quickly to external input, which reduces your ability to appropriately manage your reactions.

One thing that many people are not aware of is that the half-life of caffeine in your body is around six hours. So that means 25% of the caffeine from your 20-ounce coffee at lunchtime is still in your bloodstream at midnight, right about the time you might be wondering why you can't sleep.

Now, as with any drug, caffeine affects different people in different ways, so perhaps it doesn't affect *your* sleep, or you don't think it does, but learning about effects like this are important if you want to better understand how caffeine might be affecting your EQ.

The Impact of Sleep on EQ

Speaking of sleep, the amount of rest you get each night is both a result of, and contributes to, your emotional well-being. Research has shown that a lack of sleep can compromise your emotional well-being and that, in turn, your compromised emotional well-being can affect your sleep. If you have ever laid there at 2 a.m. staring at the ceiling feeling stressed about your workload at the office, and then had a less productive day the next day because of your lack of sleep, you'll know exactly what I mean.

How much sleep a person needs varies from one person to another, but most adults need around eight hours. The problem, though, is that time is only one factor. The quality of your sleep can also contribute to its effectiveness.

When I work with leaders to develop their emotional intelligence, I often ask how much sleep they are getting and how good that sleep is. Their answers to this question are useful source of information about their emotional well-being and it can be a good place to start when it comes to developing your EQ.

If you are having trouble sleeping, or you're not getting enough sleep, it may well be having an impact on your emotional intelligence.

Practicing sleep hygiene is a great way to start tackling this issue and many of the sleep hygiene steps are simple to implement. You will find a link to a sleep hygiene checklist in the online resources for this book.

The Impact of Alcohol on EQ

The last factor I want to discuss is alcohol. If you have ever made a bad decision, gotten into an unnecessary argument, or indulged in negative self-talk while under the influence of alcohol, it's easy to accept that this substance plays havoc with your emotional intelligence.

Research shows that alcohol can act as both a stimulant – when you are actively consuming – and a depressant – when you stop drinking and your body starts to process and eliminate it. In terms of emotional intelligence, both the run-up and run-down have an impact.

Alcohol has been proven to reduce your ability to effectively read other people's emotions, including understanding their words, tone, and body language. This is why, when two people who have been drinking start arguing, the situation often takes drastic and unexpected turns. Combined with that is the fact that alcohol affects your decision making capability, but in sometimes interesting ways.

Research shows that while under the influence of alcohol, people become less concerned with the outcomes of their decisions for themselves and for others. This is why someone who has been drinking may do things that they would never do when they are sober.

Of course, most people only drink in the evenings or on the weekend – times when they are not working. Putting aside for a second the fact that the impact of alcohol can be equally damaging in personal situations, one could be forgiven for saying that that the use of alcohol and its impact on emotional intelligence is not a concern for leaders unless they are under the influence at work.

But the big problem is that while alcohol helps you fall asleep, it significantly impairs your ability to reach REM sleep, which is the type of sleep your body and your mind need to become most rested. So, while a person may not have any alcohol in their system when they get to work the next day, their unsatisfying sleep will impact their demonstrated emotional intelligence. This is worth keeping in mind as you consider ways in which you can develop your leadership effectiveness.

Keeping Things in Perspective

Now, you might be thinking, "I thought this was a book about developing my leadership skills but now we are talking about lifestyle choices." The intention here is not to suggest you should necessarily change anything about your choices. The intent is simply to make you more aware of how these things affect your demonstrated EQ. If you are working toward developing your emotional effectiveness, these are important considerations. Also, the changes you want to make do not need to be drastic.

For example, you might choose not to consume caffeine after lunchtime, which gives your body a chance to process and eliminate it before you go to sleep. You may want to manage your alcohol intake the evening before a busy day. You may choose to drink earlier in the evening, or reduce your alcohol intake as bedtime approaches so that it gives your body a chance to eliminate the alcohol. You may want to identify situations that cause you stress and develop strategies that you can use to mitigate those stresses. And, perhaps most importantly, you may want to deliberately create sleep practices that give you the best chance of waking up healthy and refreshed.

But does it mean you will do all of these things every day, forever? Not at all. As Oscar Wilde once said, "Everything in moderation including moderation." The things we are talking about here are all personal choices. It's not necessarily about eliminating caffeine or alcohol, avoiding stressful situations, or making sure that you get eight hours of sleep every night. It's about understanding how these things impact your demonstrated emotional intelligence and your day-to-day emotional well-being, and accepting those things as part of your daily life.

Summary

If you want to reach the very highest levels of emotional effectiveness, you need to take care of yourself. While many things will affect your day-to-day emotional well-being, some of the most significant factors are sleep, alcohol, caffeine, and stress.

Understanding how each of these affects your EQ is a very important part of your leadership development practice. But as I discussed, I am not suggesting you stop drinking alcohol, or cut caffeine out of your life completely. Instead, it's about understanding the impact these things have on you, and perhaps adjusting your levels. But let's be honest, one less drink, one less cup of coffee, an hour extra of sleep, and less stress in your life is something that most people would benefit from.

Additional resources and exercises are available online at http://myeqcoach.com/lgeibook

Closing Thoughts

I want to leave you with one last observation. This is one that I share with many of the leadership groups that I work with and it's particularly important and relevant as you begin your EQ development.

The challenge for many leaders is that they are not willing to recognize that they have work to do on their leadership or that they are not willing to take the time to consider that option. These leaders, who themselves are completely fine with how things are going, will never develop their emotional intelligence because they have no interest in doing so. But for the leaders who recognize there are always things they can work to improve, and who are willing to invest the time, energy and effort to do so, the rewards can be truly worthwhile.

The important thing to remember here is that while developing your emotional intelligence is about you, the development of your emotional intelligence has the ability to positively impact everyone else in your life. Leadership, at its core, is about the experience that your followers are having of you, not necessarily the experience you are having of yourself.

Taking Your EQ Development to The Next Level

If you are interested in taking your EQ development to the next level, I encourage you to think about working with a coach and using an emotional intelligence assessment. At MyEQCoach.com, we offer coaching along with the most popular scientifically validated emotional intelligence assessment, the EQ-i 2.0, and its multi-rater version, the EQ360. As I mentioned in Chapter 6, these psychometric assessments are used to help you develop a baseline of your emotional intelligence and serve as a platform for your ongoing development.

The EQ-i is a self-reporting emotional intelligence assessment that provides you with a score for your total EI, each of the five composite scales in the EQ-i model, and all 15 subscales. You will learn about the crucial balances between key subscales as well as how aspects of emotional intelligence relate to areas of transformational leadership. You will also learn about specific leadership derailers that can prevent you from reaching your full leadership potential.

The EQ-i takes about 20 minutes to complete and is debriefed with you, one-on-one, as part of a short- or long-term coaching package.

The EQ360 is a multi-rater, 360-degree assessment of your EQ-i. It provides all the same information as the EQ-i, but it allows you to collect feedback from up to 5 groups of raters, such as managers, peers, family, and friends. The information collected from these groups is compared to the ratings that you gave yourself across all 15 subscales of the EQ-i model. This allows you to identify allied strengths, blind spots, and jointly acknowledged opportunities for growth, across the entire spectrum of emotional intelligence. The EQ360 also allows you to collect free text feedback through five completely customizable questions, further increasing its value as a leadership development tool.

We administer and debrief hundreds of these assessments every year and have extensive experience in helping leaders use their reports as part of their EQ development.

EQ Coaching Packages

For our corporate clients we provide the EQ-i and EQ360 assessments as part of workshops and larger leadership development programs. For individuals, we offer assessments as part of a range of EQ coaching packages that include both the assessment and coaching sessions.

As someone who has read The Leader's Guide to Emotional Intelligence, you will automatically receive a 10% discount on any of our assessment and coaching packages if you sign up. Just drop me an email – info@myeqcoach.com, and let me know you read this book. I will arrange for the discount.

Final Note

So, that's the Leader's Guide to Emotional Intelligence. I hope you enjoyed reading it as much as I enjoyed writing it. My goal in this book was to provide you with a solid understanding of what emotional intelligence is, as well as a practical and meaningful approach to developing it. If you apply the processes I covered in this book, you CAN become a more emotionally effective leader, and the world needs more of those!

Over the past 10 years I have seen how leaders with a high level of emotional intelligence get some amazing results. The kind of results I am talking about is not woo-woo fuzzy stuff. They are things like higher productivity, improved team culture, reduced sick time, and lower turnover.

Leaders who are willing to take the time and expend the effort to understand and develop their emotional intelligence stand apart from their peers. They experience the kind of success that most leaders want, but few are willing to do the work needed to get there.

Do the work. Remember it's for the benefit of others just as much as it is for you. That's the nature and character of great leadership.

Additional resources and exercises are available online at http://myeqcoach.com/lgeibook

About the Author

Drew Bird is an established leadership and organizational development practitioner with more than a decade of experience coaching leaders, developing programs, and creating leadership and development solutions that generate results. He has experience working with leaders, coaches, consultants, and organizations of all sizes. With more than 25 years of experience working in and with some of the world's most well-known organizations, Drew has experienced and witnessed first-hand the difference that effective leaders and effective leadership practices can have on an organization and the people within it.

He is a Premier Partner and an approved Certifying Trainer for the EQ-i and EQ360 instruments by Multi-Health Systems (MHS), as well as the Risk Type Compass assessment and the Pearman Personality Integrator. In addition, he holds certifications as an Achieve Global Master Trainer, is a qualified MBTI practitioner, and is certified in the Mayer Salovey Caruso Emotional Intelligence Test (MSCEIT) as well as the Hogan HDS, HPI, and MVPI instruments.

Drew holds an MSc in Organizational Psychology from the University of London, England, and an MA in Leadership from Royal Roads University in Victoria, Canada. He is a member of the Canadian Psychological Society (CPA) and the Society for Industrial and Organizational Psychology (SIOP).

Through his company, ClearPoint Leadership Strategies (http://www.clearpointleadership.com/), he provides emotional intelligence related products and services to leaders, coaches, consultants, and organizations.

An accomplished speaker, Drew uses his interactive, engaging style as a way to draw from his real-world organizational experience. Drew helps individuals in the audience see their own role in creating vibrant, healthy teams and productive and engaging workplaces. Participants leave his sessions with practical, actionable advice that they can use to become more emotionally effective. With experience speaking to groups both large and small, Drew tailors his presentations to audiences of all sizes for maximum impact.

If you'd like to learn more about the projects Drew is working on or speak with him directly, don't hesitate to reach out.

Email: drew@clearpointleadership.com
Twitter: @drew_bird
LinkedIn: https://ca.linkedin.com/in/drewbird

Made in the USA
Monee, IL
03 March 2021